TH
CULT
PHENOM

THE CULTIC PHENOMENON

A REVEALING LOOK AT OURSELVES

Dan'l Markham

An Albatross Book

Published in Australia by
Albatross Books Pty Ltd
PO Box 320, Sutherland
NSW 2232, Australia
and in the United Kingdom by
Lion Publishing
Icknield Way, Tring
Herts HP23 4LE, England

First edition 1987

National Library of Australia
Cataloguing-in-Publication data

Markham, Dan'l C
The Cultic Phenomenon

Simultaneously published: Tring, Herts:
Lion Publishing
ISBN 0 86760 029 2 (Albatross)
ISBN 0 85648 1184 6 (Lion)

1. Cults. I. Title. (Series: Issues for the times).

289.9.009'4

Cover photo: Wildlight Photo Agency
Bondi Beach, NSW 2026, Australia
Typeset by Rochester Photosetting Service, Sydney
Printed by Globe Press Pty Ltd, Melbourne

Contents

Foreword

In recent years, cults and new religious movements have been something of a growth industry in the West. Assorted gurus, self-proclaimed messiahs and religious teachers have invaded the turf of traditional Christianity. As the author rightly points out, Christian churches themselves have not been immune to one form or another of cultism.

One of the strengths of this book is that it encourages us to look at the cultic phenomenon in broad perspective. Evangelical Christians especially have tended to view cults largely from a theological vantage point. While doctrinal considerations are paramount for the Christian and are addressed in the pages of this book, it is equally important to examine the social and psychological roots and causes of cultism. This book helps us to do just that. It underscores the right of every person — whatever his or her religious affiliation or inclination — to cherish and to guard the freedom to choose and the freedom to hear. It warns of the abuses — spiritual, psychological, and interpersonal — which are the hallmarks of religious totalitarianism.

God's adversary is active as never before in his campaign to seduce the unsuspecting. It is my prayer that whoever reads this book will be assisted in developing the discernment skills so necessary in confronting and understanding today's incredible spiritual marketplace.

Ronald Enroth, Ph.D.
Professor of Sociology
Westmont College
Santa Barbara, California
USA

Acknowledgements

Scripture quotations marked NAS used by permission from the *New American Standard Bible*, © The Lockman Foundation, 1960, 1962, 1963, 1971, 1972, 1973, 1975, 1977, Lahabra, California.

Scripture quotations marked NIV are taken from the *Holy Bible, New International Version*, © 1973, 1978, 1984, New York International Bible Society.

Scripture quotations marked TLB are taken from *The Living Bible*,© 1971 by Tyndale House Publishers, Wheaton, Illinois. Used by permission.

Scripture quotations marked KJV are taken from the *King James Version*.

An annotated bibliography of literature related to new religious movements is reprinted by kind permission of Spiritual Counterfeits Project Inc., © 1980, 1984, PO Box 4398, Berkeley, CA 94704, USA.

Resources relevant to religious cults in Australia is reprinted by kind permission of J.L.F. Buchner, Lecturer, Macarthur Institute of Higher Education, PO Box 108 Milperra, NSW 2214, Australia.

I wish to thank my good friend Peter Stahl who provided perceptive insight, solid research and diligent editing; Louise Nelson who gave of her time to edit and encourage; and my wife Kathie who has by her spiritual support enabled me to write this book.

Dan'l Markham

1

A look at our environment

NOVEMBER 18, 1978 was a day of infamy which should stand vividly in our minds as a memorial, a lesson, a warning; a day that jolted much of the world into stupefied bewilderment; a day hundreds of innocent and sincere yet brainwashed people ended their lives at the command of megalomaniac Jim Jones of Jonestown, Guyana.

A need for balance

'If I have learned anything from Jonestown,' warns Mel White, author of a book on the People's Temple tragedy, 'it is that those events could happen again.'[1]

More than an outrageous tragedy, it was a bizarre, macabre nightmare. Yet we tend to think that Jonestown was only a rare, extreme occurrence. Rare? Extreme? Hardly. Billy Graham has said it is estimated there are 2,000 self-proclaimed messiahs in the United States.[2] Professor Ronald Enroth of Westmont College, who is one of the nation's leading cult authorities, has stated to me that there are some 1,300 cults in the USA alone. He emphasises that this is a conservative estimate. In 1979, NBC stated that approximately eight million Americans were deceived by cults.[3] Keep in mind concerning this phenomenon that the US is only a microcosm of the rest of the world. No nation is exempt from the cult epidemic.

To qualify our concern further, Doctor Walter Martin of Christian Research Institute, perhaps one of the most

1 Mel White, *Deceived*, Fleming H. Revell Co., New Jersey: 1979, p.11

2 Billy Graham, 'Signs of His Coming', *Decision*, Billy Graham Evangelistic Association, November 1980, p.2

3 Mel White, ibid.

outspoken critics and prolific authors on cults, recently declared an estimate of thirty-four million cultists in the United States. In addition, Dr Martin accurately predicted that Bhagwan Shree ('Sir God') Rajneesh, a controversial leader and guru to 250,000 devoted followers from some twenty-two nations, would become the guru of the nineteen eighties. Just as Dr Martin accurately foresaw the disaster that came to the People's Temple and Jonestown years before it occurred, he now says the same end will come to people in some other cults. 'The US will have more Guyanas', he said in July 1982 in an address at a Christian festival in Vancouver, Washington State.

Ron Carlson, president of Christian Ministries International, and widely recognised as an outstanding lecturer on the subject of non-Christian cults, estimates less conservatively than Enroth that there are between three and four thousand cults in the US alone, and that seventy-eight per cent of the members of these cults come from mainline Christianity.

What catapults the cultic issue into a new realm of concern is the fact that so much has been published, filmed, tape-recorded and said of cults that our society may easily become lulled into attitudes of indifference. When over half of the publicity centres around the sensational rather than the analytical and critical reporting of the cultic phenomenon, it leaves the public with considerable fear and/or disgust, and with little preparation for dealing with cults, dealing with friends who belong to cults, or protecting themselves from cultic seduction.

Sadly, most of today's cults will probably become gradually accepted by most of society. It has happened already. Several religious groups that were considered cults in the nineteenth century are today considered mainstream religions. The Unification Church, a more recent movement regarded as a cult by a general consensus of the news media and Christian organisations, recently pushed a propaganda programme for its acceptance. Another large sect started in America, the worldwide Church of Jesus Christ of Latter-day Saints (Mormons), long considered a cult by cult authorities such as Dr Walter Martin, has already gained social acceptance through the efforts of zealous missionaries, huge budgets, political clout and worldwide advertising campaigns.

The astonishing proliferation of cults in the last ten years proves the susceptibility of our culture to the cultic phenomenon. If one examines the Jim Jones People's Temple story and other cultic movements, one finds it is not just the poor, the disadvantaged, the uneducated, the young or the elderly who are deceived by cults, but lawyers, doctors, and other professionals, lettered in almost every academic field imaginable. The point is that few people are fully prepared to deal personally with cults. Therefore it is imperative that whether we are Christians, atheists, liberals or fundamentalists, we should seriously begin to educate ourselves about the reasons behind the growing acceptance of cults, their proliferation, and our susceptibility to them.

It is also imperative that we approach this highly emotional and inflammatory controversy with balanced perspectives. We must never forget that while a cult may appear to be an evil, elitist, separatist, intolerant, and abusive group, it is a gathering made up of real people such as ourselves, who have genuine needs and sincere reasons for belonging. While millions already suffer spiritually, mentally and socially at the hands of cultic groups, thousands more will find themselves becoming loyal cult adherents if we are apathetic or unaware of the roots and causes in society that drive people towards cults. Such people have admirable goals and high ideals, and they must be approached and treated with both perception and truth, and with sensitivity, understanding, and compassion. We must be careful how we deal with the cultic phenomenon, and it will certainly not be by becoming elitist, separatist, intolerant or abusive ourselves.

A proper awareness requires an understanding of cults' roots and causes. We can point fingers and say, 'That's bad!' never thinking that we could possibly be responsible in some way. In following the dictates of our own philosophies, theologies and attitudes, or lack of them, we may be actually contributing to the type of environment in which cults flourish.

Eliminating the weaknesses in society that give opportunities to cults may mean looking inside ourselves and examining our own motives for forming social relationships.

But before we can do that we must focus on the fact we have been, are, and always will be social creatures. Because of our natural make-up, social groups are a basic part of our existence. Consequently, one or a few persons or groups will always be attempting to influence, lead or control us as we become members of groups. Our membership of whatever groups we join or find ourselves in will isolate and insulate us. Belonging, while it provides psychological and sociological security, to some extent controls the amount of knowledge available to us about ourselves and others. Limited knowledge provides a fertile place for the growth of abuses of others and ourselves, abuses such as bigotry, racism, elitism, and self-deception.

Ending social relationships altogether is not the solution! We desire order and security in our lives. Without social relationships there is no social order, and that leaves us with chaos, which is the first step for those who wish to take advantage of power. Hitler, Lenin and their disciples created chaos in order to gain totalitarian power. So our hope is not to become non-social or anti-social beings; it is to learn how to form and maintain social groups correctly, whether they are economical, spiritual or other groups.

I want to emphasise that today's cultic tragedies are not simple problems with simple answers; they are the products of a complex environment. Their victims are not simply a deceived group of zealots led and controlled by a diabolical leader. My goal is to help you not only in spotting cults but also in seeing their roots and causes in your own environment. To do this I will be trying to make you aware of our social weaknesses and needs, with the final goal of enabling you to learn how to minister properly to those needs and weaknesses.

Adjusting our viewpoint

Christians often believe that they are immune to cultic influences, reasoning that if one is a Christian, one automatically cannot be in a cult. Investigation reveals the opposite: many cults, a good case example being the People's Temple, have had and do have sincere, truly dedicated

Christians as members. Deeply religious people are highly susceptible to the cults' lure.

Furthermore, Christians frequently say things like, 'Well, if God didn't want those people to be in a cult and if their hearts were open to the Lord, then they wouldn't be deceived.' Yet their criteria for determining what is or is not cultic needs readjustment. It used to be that Christians determined a group's cultic leanings solely on the basis of its ability or inability to line up with historically accepted denominational doctrines or orthodox statements of faith. This system is worthy of use, but it has weaknesses. What about groups who have correct statements of faith but abuse their members? Some people have argued, with merit, that this historical procedure is subjective and self-serving in determining a cult, since established denominations can simply exclude any group with views opposing their own. As we shall see, today's complex picture requires refined methods for evaluating religious sects.

We may also be blind to the fact that many cults today are founded on other factors besides religious and theological doctrines. While religious cults receive extensive media attention we are often distracted from the fact that sporting, financial, political, and personality cults abound around us. Cultism is in every aspect of life. We are in an age of cultism. We need not go far to find sport groupies or rock star groupies as well as groups dedicated to financial causes, dietary pursuits, para-psychological disciplines, and occultic followings, all of which do their share of inflicting abuses.

Using his sociological expertise, Professor Ronald Enroth has introduced a refined mode of recognising cults. He explains that every cult, despite its apparent uniqueness among other cults, has various signs, patterns, actions, and philosophies which remain constant for all cults. For instance, every cult inflicts sociological abuses on its members. Some are intentional and others are not. Five primary ones are: abuse of time, abuse of money, abuse of intimacy, abuse of authority, and abuse of sexuality. These may be inflicted upon members in varying degrees depending on the cultic situation, but every cult has been found to practice at least a majority of these abuses.

A cult then is any group with an elitist cause and view of itself that in order to promote its cause either consciously or unconsciously abuses individuals' rights and freedoms. The crucial point in determining that a group is a cult is whether or not the individual members have their wills violated, overpowered or coerced into total submission and control. This means a religious group could possibly adhere to orthodox doctrines and still be a cult because of the abuses it inflicts on members. Many people — even knowledgeable ones — believe that to be a cult an organisation must be controlled by hypnosis, personality worship or neutralising chants. Such tactics are employed by some of the less sophisticated cults; cults generally have more subtle methods of operation.

This subtlety is effectively deceptive in many cases. It is not a case of evil mental prowess and treacherous cunning but one in which both leaders and abused followers sincerely believe in their cause. That dedication, however holy in their view, has produced a justification system where the ends do (unfortunately) justify the means, even if the means are abusive, sinful or unethical. It is difficult to help a person from a group like this clearly see that others' points of view are just as valid as his own when he 'knows' for certain he alone is right. In his concrete determination there is no greater cause than his elitist cause.

When identifying a group as cultic it is important to remember that nearly every group that manifests these social characteristics also fails to measure up to certain orthodox doctrines. For example, in *The Mindbenders*, Jack Sparks notes that The Way International (a fast-growing sect Sparks exposes as a pseudo-Christian cult) inflicts financial abuses on its members, besides teaching that Jesus is not God. 'Everything costs in The Way,' he reveals, especially the numerous courses members are pressured to take.[4]

Again let me emphasise that today's cultic phenomenon is not a simple problem with simple answers. For example, terrorist groups are often not viewed as being cultic, but their

---

4 Jack Sparks, *The Mindbenders*, Thomas Nelson Inc., New York: 1977, p.20

narrow ideologies and the control they exercise over members' thoughts and actions strongly imply cultism. Totalitarian regimes which exercise rigid control over the minds of the masses give a wider picture of our cult-plagued world.

Often in a cultic atmosphere a total willingness to serve the cause means a total obedience to the group's leaders. The members' belief in the cause becomes so overwhelmingly intertwined with their belief in the group and its leaders that the leader's voice to the cultist becomes the actual voice of the cause; therefore, the leaders can do no wrong no matter how much they exact from members and no matter how unethical their actions in gaining new members have become. Individuality is lost to the extent that the cultist no longer has any personal responses and interactions with the world; thoughts and philosophies are no longer separate from group thinking. The cultist reacts to society only as the group would react.

In the preceding paragraph I have used the term 'the cause' several times, but other terms such as God, The Revolution or The Party may be substituted for the object of the cultists' commitment, to show that cultism is not a simple deviation of the over-zealous 'religious' mind.

Yet the tragic fact is that religious-psychological cults can reach far deeper into the minds of their adherents, abuse them far more, and make them even more susceptible to total control than social-political cults can. While political cults (totalitarian regimes) have imposed far-reaching controls and use a variety of tools to manipulate the masses under them, they often fall short of completely taking away one's autonomy or wholly controlling one's will. As terrible as totalitarianism is (either the far right or the far left), it is usually less mentally abusive and injurious than religious totalitarianism, and it is far less seductive and subtle. Mixing religious and governmental control, Ayatollah Khomeini has produced one of the greatest cultic societies in the modern world.

Religious cults in the name of God or Christ often receive total yielding of the adherent's will. Because the cult's cause is understood by its members to be the absolute cause of God they will often give eagerly all finances, assets, energies, and time to the group in its efforts to bring its revelation to the world. As mentioned earlier, cult adherents and their leaders often sincerely believe in their calling and cause. It is this sincere commitment and dedication that makes it so difficult to reach even greatly abused cult members.

Now that we have seen how deeply cultism reaches into the everyday world around us we are ready to investigate some roots and causes of the cultic phenomenon.

Roots and causes

No single cause of cultism is as pervading as the need to belong. As a social creature, mankind has always had this deep craving for acceptance and recognition — to make a mark on his society and assure himself a place in history; to be a part of *the* cause whatever it might be.

Author-psychologist Dr Lawrence J. Crabb, Jnr, in his book *Basic Principles of Biblical Counseling*, declares that mankind's two basic needs are security and significance.[5] Today in the western world these needs are chronic because of the disintegration of authority and order in the family unit and because of the loss of other longstanding social and moral-spiritual standards. The contemporary, widely accepted philosophy of relativism proclaims, basically, that what is the right and the norm for today is what society says is the right and the norm, and that tomorrow's right and norm will be what tomorrow's society will decide then. Thus, consistent standards, accepted by all, are gone, leaving mankind with no standards higher than his own present standards of morality; so he is left with little stability as he tries to determine his individual value in a world of values that are constantly changing around him. Insecurity has become one of mankind's most serious epidemics. It is, unfortunately, not recognised as such.

Traditionally, man has followed and strived for goals and standards higher than himself that have kept him from slipping further into the relativism of his own standards. Western civilisation has (until the last century) been guided by Judeo-Christian ethics which are higher than man himself,

---

5 Lawrence J. Crabb, Jr, *Basic Principles of Biblical Counseling*, Zondervan, Michigan: 1975, p.62

and by absolutes greater than his own comprehension. These provided western mankind with a secure judge for his actions, a secure view of the future, and a secure base for forming relationships: God and his revelation, the Bible.

What this breakdown of standards and goals has done is to leave society with philosophies that broadly speaking have no secure answers, no significant goals and few or no lofty standards. The result is tremendous insecurities for social beings. Many people, especially young people, desire to find meaning to life. In searching for significance, in reaching for something with clear, secure answers, they find that the authoritative, firmly believed goals of cults feed their deep cravings, for the security they feel has been denied them by past abuses.

Yes, cults and their various causes give adherents meaning for their existence and offer them the love and purpose they desperately need. As a part of the cultic group, the member has a sure calling and purpose in life freed from the confusion of today's varied and often nebulous philosophies. Many ex-cultists have said they were drawn to the cult because of the overwhelming personal love they were given by cult members. Many ex-members of the Unification Church have attested to this powerful influence of love.

It is not too hard to figure out why this love is so effective, considering family decay and our rushing, mechanised, brusque, and indifferent society. In addition, sociologists and psychologists tell us we are in a 'me-society'; we are extremely preoccupied with self. We are a selfish society full of members who have not received the proper amount of the greatest emotional need of all: love. Love is only truly understood, received, and enjoyed by those who *give* of themselves (in other words love others), declares Dr Leo Buscagalia in his challenging and convicting book *Love*.[6]

Many of the severest critics of cults frequently fail to recognise that the love expressed between cult members and the leaders is not just a tactic. Leaders often have actually deceived themselves; consequently, a genuine love and a personal caring relationship bonds the group together with

6 Leo Buscagalia, *Love*, Fawcett Crest Books, New York: 1972

the leader, especially when they perceive themselves and their leader as being objects of persecution. An enemy, whether real or imagined, produces the best of any group committed to one another and a cause.

Cult books consistently reveal that young and old alike are drawn into deep commitments to their cults because of an intimate warm fellowship, a close-knit family-type relationship. In discussing the reason for being so deeply affected by the cults' expressions of love, many ex-cultists noted that they had never received the personal love and attention they needed from their families or their childhood churches — a sad indictment against those churches.

While many established churches and denominations have felt the sting of proselytising efforts by successful cults, such churches and their individual members would do well to allow the success of the cultic evangelising to move them to serious self-examination as to how well they themselves are living out I Corinthians 13 (the love chapter) and Christ's two great commandments: to love the Lord, and to love others as you love yourself. Churches, ministers, and all Christians are left with piercing challenges. How far are we ourselves responsible for the cultic phenomenon?

Another often listed reason for the attractiveness of cults is the members' sincere dedication to the group's beliefs and high standards of morality. The strongest critics of Sun Myung Moon's Unification Church cannot deny that he has produced a deeply dedicated, sincerely moral group of people. Again, the Christian churches stand challenged.

A third reflection of society's insecurities, especially as far as young people are concerned, is the deep-seated desire for a strong, authoritative leadership, particularly a strong parental influence. Cultic leaders, the majority of whom are males, provide clear, authoritative, and thus secure direction for young, fertile, yet apprehensive minds facing uncertain futures in a foreboding, confusing and often crazy world. Ages eighteen to twenty-five have proved to be the group most susceptible to the cultic lure and its provisions. Youthful uninitiated minds easily fall prey to the strong figure who provides clear black and white answers for society's multitude of perplexing and complex problems.

There are more contributing factors which cause proliferation of cults, but this short analysis of roots an causes should give us an adequate understanding so that we may continue.

The subtlety of cultism

Recognising an organisation as being cultic may not be as easy as one might think. A legitimate group can be mistaken for a cult, and an aberrant group can be mistaken for being legitimate. For instance, because People's Temple and Jim Jones falsified biblically-defined gifts of the Holy Spirit such as speaking in tongues, prophecy and healing, other Christian groups who profess to have such gifts could, therefore, be labelled unjustly as cults, with the opposite occurring when cults use a Christian front and are perceived as legitimate.

Certainly there are obvious cultic groups that blatantly stand out: eastern imported cults such as Divine Light Mission and the Unification Church. These groups are foreign to the western mind and create suspicion. Because of their unfamiliarity they are quickly recognised. But other cultic groups are more subtle.

Researchers from Spiritual Counterfeits Project, a Berkeley-based Christian organisation that analyses cults, noted that worship services at the People's Temple emphasised 'Fundamentalist-Pentecostal Christian trappings and biblical language'.[7] While viewed by some with caution and concern, Jim Jones and People's Temple in its beginning stages was not seen by most as being the cult it now so obviously was. In fact, those who first attempted to expose People's Temple were often not taken seriously because Jones had built such an effective and positive image of himself and his following. The Temple had a Christian appearance. Jones was ordained by a respected and accepted denomintion, the Disciples of Christ.[8] According to the testimonies from ex-members of People's Temple, Jones not only fooled people, but used a Methodist superintendent to gain and maintain respect-

7 Mel White, op.cit., pp.39-40

8 Mel White, ibid.

So Jones purposely put on a front not only to public into thinking the Temple was legitimately ...n, but also to attract Christians to his church.

...view the definition of a cult, I have said it is any group ...n elitist, unique cause and view of itself which, while ...oting its cause consciously or unconsciously, abuses the personal rights and freedoms of individuals. *Abuse* is the key determining factor.

Sparks (*The Mindbenders*) and Enroth (*The Lure of the Cults*) list some of what they consider the more prominent Christian aberrational groups. But what about the numerous aberrational Christian groups that have not been so prominently labelled a cult? Since some cults may have a surface that appears legitimate, how can you determine whether questionable groups in your own community are cultic? As pointed out, there are numerous sociological indicators and patterns which identify a group as being potentially cultic. A knowledge of a few of these indicators will assist you in forming your own decisions:

1. Leaders who claim a unique, exclusive ministry, revelation or position of authority from God.
2. A belief that the group is the only true church (group) or that it maintains a critical stance regarding Christianity while it praises and exalts its own leader's ministry consistently.
3. Use of intimidation by warning that members who leave the group will 'go to hell' or suffer some other calamity.
4. The *requirement* that members give substantial portions of their income to the group or leaders.
5. Emphasis on loyalty to the group that results in almost total absorption of one's life into its activities.
6. The fact that ministries of the group and its individual members are inseparable from the ministries of the leaders.
7. Control by leaders of group members' private lives.
8. Discouraging of dissent and any questioning of the leaders' teachings or directives. Criticism, even if

9 Mel White, op.cit., p.183

constructive, is seen as rebellion. Emphasis on authority, obedience and submission are vigilantly maintained.
9. Expectations that loyalty to the leaders and to the group will be clearly demonstrated.
10. Confrontations by present adherents of any who leave the group in order to encourage or coerce them back into the group's control.

As Enroth noted, 'The loss of true autonomy, the manipulation and ultimate subversion of the will, and the surrender of the mind to the group are all hallmarks of cultic control.'[10]

These cultic indicators are not exhaustive, and just one or even a few will not necessarily determine that a group is cultic; but questions should be raised and caution suggested if a group you are examining does exhibit one or more of them.

The abused cult adherent

The effects of cults on the individual can be devastating — psychologically, socially, and even physically. The results are numerous, and include personality changes, loss of identity, paranoia and social disorientation. From the previous list of ten indicators I have extracted a smaller list of abuses the individual will experience in a cult:

1. Abuse of individuality and the development of a group mentality.
2. Abuse of intimacy. Relationships with friends, parents, children and even spouses are broken or seriously hindered by the development of a 'we versus them' mentality that makes outsiders evil enemies of the cause.
3. Abuse of money. Threatening demands with peer group pressure drain off large portions of a member's income, causing financial neglect of self and perhaps family.
4. Abuse of time. The group soon controls and uses most of one's time, often leaving the member in a constant state of exhaustion.

---

10 Ronald M. Enroth, *The Lure of the Cults*, Herald Books, New York: 1979

5. Abuse of will. Adherents unquestioningly submit to the demands and controls of the group's leaders.

No one can truly understand the psychological and emotional turmoil or the resultant physical effects experienced by abused cult members better than cult defectors and a few of the people who aid such persons. A cult defector from a group in Washington State related to me that while ethically and mentally he knew he had made the right decision in leaving his highly authoritarian group, the separation and ensuing loss of direction, along with other results of abuse, left him frequently weeping (sometimes uncontrollably) months and even years after his defection.

Marriage and other intimate relationships must be repaired or often totally rebuilt. Some marriages have been and will be unable to stand the stress of social, emotional, financial and personality readjustments. Only time will tell what the overall effects upon children involved in such struggles will be. Many lives have been totally shattered; sanity, purpose in life, and even desire to live have been lost. Suicide is common.

When asked why they did not leave the People's Temple when things began to go from bad to terrible, numerous members replied, 'Where could we go?' Most cult defectors face the same dilemma of uncertainty, fear, and disorientation.

Ex-cultists must wage a personal war with guilt, humiliation, and lack of self-esteem. My hope is that they can look at their experience in the wider picture of their entire life and realise they still have much to offer society from their experience, and that their lessons can steer them and others into a better, richer, more meaningful life. Often those who have gone through deprivation can more fully appreciate life's freedoms and responsibilities and other blessings that the rest of us often take for granted. Such people also have a greater opportunity in showing compassion for others who hurt.

Of primary concern to us all is that thousands of human beings in America and around the globe are losing the most precious of all rights — the right and freedom of the individual to choose: the freedom of the individual will. Cultic control denies such choosing of one's own destiny. In fact cultic religions in the USA violate the heart of the legal right that protects them. Out of malice and greed, or out of ignorant sincerity, by thought manipulation and group control they deny their members the 'free exercise' of religion the First Amendment guarantees.

Another example of abuse is when the 'freedom to hear' is violated. Once locked into a cult, the member's total philosophic outlook on religion, politics, history, psychology, biology, economics, sociology etc., is dictated to him by the leader. The reading of literature and the teaching of anything outside the group's belief system is forbidden or at least heavily frowned upon. This disapproval is efficiently enforced by peer group pressure.

As for social abuse, the adherents' legitimate needs such as family activities, personal relationships and individual hopes are scheduled out by a priority list of more important 'spiritual works' to be accomplished for the cause of the group. Work, businesses and recreational enjoyment frequently suffer.

Psychologically, the process is not usually blatant brainwashing, but either persuasion or gradual coercion. This is a long (sometimes extremely long) and subtle process. It ends with the follower yielding all or most of his personal decision-making and opinion-forming processes to the leaders; they in his mind are more spiritual and have more divine wisdom. One pastor in a questionable church admonished his congregation (after years of building up a thorough authority doctrine around himself) in the following words: 'You have no right to hold your own opinion — only a right to God's opinion.' The congregation responded with hearty 'Amens' in agreement, not seeing it was, and is, the pastor who solely decided what 'God's opinions' were. The most disturbing fact is that this two thousand-strong congregation of agreers included lawyers, doctors and other skilled professionals whose work requires them to have discerning minds.

Again, I want to stress that no one type of person is completely immune from the allurements of the cultic phenomenon.

Emotionally the pain experienced by those who begin to question or who do actually leave a cult is excruciating. Imagine losing *all* your close friends and contacts in one day. Chastisement for being out of line with the leaders generally ends by members being directed to cut the questioning adherent off from all contact. Following this act, if excommunication is continued, in many cases the targeted individual is threatened with misfortune, either from the group or from 'God' via the group. For example, one couple left a large 'church' because of sexual confrontations made by the group's leader toward the wife. In attempting to restrain the couple from leaving the group, the leader's wife warned, 'Well, honey, you know that some people who get out of God's will, God has taken them home.' (God has killed them.) To the adherent this type of threat is real and frightening. The brainwashed and confused adherents will reason that perhaps they are going against God by disobeying their leader.

As previously mentioned, once a person leaves a cult, crushing emotional and physical pain resulting from confusion, guilt and fear can go on for months or years, even a lifetime. The ex-cultist often drifts in an unstable emotional-mental state. This confusing, lost state is understandable since nearly all social, psychological and spiritual reference points the former cultist had are left behind with the group while the friends he had before entering the cult may treat his return to his original environment with only an 'I told you so' atmosphere of abuse. In this weak emotional state, finding new direction in a world with unfamiliar beliefs and goals is an awesome, painful and difficult task.

Another closely related mental state which author-psychologist Flo Conway entitles 'snapping' also plagues the cult escapee.[11] He might feel free and believe his decision to leave the group was correct; his reasoning takes over as facts dictate the past cultic experience *was* wrong. But sooner or later strong emotions cloud his certainty again; guilt and fear stimulated by months and years of cultic programming take over. Badgered and abused, his mind tormented with conflicts, confusions and swirling emotions, the escapee 'snaps' back into an emotional dependence on the cult; the

---

11 Flo Conway and Jim Siegleman, *Snapping*, Dell Publishing Co., New York: 1979, p.13

previous certainty of belief in the cult, however wrong, overrides the factual evidence of its abusive actions. During this 'snapping' process the ex-member is extremely susceptible to repeated attempts by the group or its emissaries to draw him back under the cult's influence and dominion.

Keep in mind that most attempts to bring the refugee back are carried out by deeply sincere and loving cult members who were the escapee's former companions. These rescuers actually believe they are performing an honourable, spiritual deed in saving the escapee, their former companion, from deception, darkness or some other sombre ending. This sincerity and loving concern makes it all the more difficult for the refugee to resist returning.

As can be surmised, there is a desperate need in the ex-cultist for consistent and positive reinforcement. This is a reinforcement of genuine, loving, sensitive and yet firm corrective information by friends and relatives who are knowledgeable about the cultic phenomenon.

Cultic authority

One of the most significant factors contributing to the absolute authority that cultic leaders can exercise is the contemporary challenge to traditional authority roles within our society. A misuse of power in the past two decades has led people to distrust persons of authority; furthermore, laws have been seen as a legalised system of abuse for keeping in power those persons or institutions that already dominate society. It is this loss of trust for traditional standards and ensuing disrespect for authority figures over the last twenty years that has left many people in our society with a neurosis: an over-dependent psychological need for firm guidelines and strong directives.

Responding to what they saw as a breakdown of authority, some leaders, including those of religious prominence, felt they had to emphasise heavily the need for teaching submission to authority. In the early seventies a wave of authority-instruction in Christian churches, especially in conservative Christian circles, rushed upon the religious scene. For example, a popular Christian seminar leader who primarily deals with authority teaches Christians to obey Christian leaders even if as individuals they believe particular directives are wrong or the leader is wrong. This teacher mistakenly reasons that if a person obeys his or her immediate leader, such as husband, employer or pastor, the leader not the follower is the one who is solely responsible before God for the sin or wrong committed as the result of an improper directive. This leaves non-leaders to assume it is better and safer to obey blindly than to decide anything for themselves. 'I'm not responsible for my decisions, my leader is.' Under this system it is said to be better to obey and sin than to disobey and reason for oneself.

In this rapid swing from authority rejection to enforcement of authority roles, both cultic and non-cultic groups have found it easier to gain complete control over a group of people by providing them with a strong religious hierarchy and a single leader whose unquestioned authority will lead the group safely through the indecisive environment that a society with relatively non-absolute standards creates. Followers' obedience will insure their protection, leaders claim; after all, Paul, Peter, and even Popes have had the right to rule with absolute authority (or have they?). They adamantly believe the scriptures give them, as shepherds or pastors over their flocks, positions of absolute authority. We shall see that the scriptures teach the contrary.

The solution to this neurosis (the need for firm guidelines and strong directives) is not absolute control over everyone by a few people or a single individual; yet authority and order are still needed. Society is always struggling to find order, and hence both authority and follower roles, without surrendering to extremes, are necessary.

Cultic leaders criticise shared authority and shared power such as democratic rule for being cumbersome and inefficient – slow in action and results. True, democratic rule is slower and in some cases more inefficient than totalitarian rule. But what is more valuable, the degree of efficiency or the degree of safety in protecting inalienable rights that constitutions – such as the US Constitution and the Bill of Rights – ensure? Given over to abuses, the efficiency thought to be gained through totalitarianism will always turn into an abused, unhealthy society which degenerates into a total lack of efficiency, Poland's economy being a clear example.

Democratic/constitutional governments with a balance of powers clearly recognise this tension between authority and follower roles. Constitutional power granted by the people to the few while being checked by divisions of power strikes at the heart of man's susceptibility to power abuse and hopefully guides societies and individuals away from extremes.

The rise of the cultic phenomenon in the twentieth century suggests society is losing the struggle to religious and political totalitarianism.

Dr Paul Tournier, a noted Christian writer, explains that professionals such as doctors, social workers, psychologists and ministers have chosen vocations of power, and that all such people need to be aware of the temptations to control, manipulate, and even exploit. He says, '...there is in us, especially in those whose intentions are of the purest, an excessive and destructive will to power which eludes even the most sincere and honest self-examination.'[12]

Unfortunately, when someone is a leader — professing to be a Christian minister or some other type of spiritual leader — other people naively think he has divine ordination and is not susceptible to the allurements of power. Yet as a pastor myself, I have been appalled to find how many people were eager to exalt me, and due to my position I was, in their eyes, nearly perfect in spiritual matters. It is not surprising that the Roman Catholic church found itself first believing and then teaching that when the Pope speaks 'ex-cathedra' he does so without fault.

So the problem rests not only with a careful use of power by those to whom it has been delegated or yielded, but also with those who would give more power to their leaders for the sake of security. We as followers must resist the temptations to exalt or subtly worship those whom we choose to follow. Admiration and desire to be like someone else can easily drift into the realm of worship — meaning that we can make our leaders cultic by our own actions or by our docility.

At first the worship of an individual is not always done outwardly. It begins with subtle attitudes of admiration in the

---

12 Ronald M. Enroth, 'The Power Abusers', *Eternity*, Evangelistic Ministries Inc., Pennsylvania: 1979, p.25

mind. What one may call admiration or desire to emulate others may actually be worship in its most common form. Given the opportunity, the cultic leader with autocratic rule may feed that simple, sincere admiration of his authoritative personality until it grows into total worship of himself by his followers.

To those of us who hope to treat our neuroses simply, the leader promises quick remedies that are not really cures but are only another stage of our illnesses. The leader has not cured our over-dependent need for firm guidelines and strong directives. On the contrary, he would tell us that we are not ill at all, but that we are an elite and separate group from the rest of society that he has been called to lead.

Various accepted Christian groups are often responsible for fuelling aberrant authority doctrines which cultic leaders are quick to employ. One example on the fringes of mainstream Christianity, for example, which certain groups have accepted and then pushed, is a doctrine of authority called *discipling*.

Pastor Chuck Smith of Costa Mesa, California, who is a noted Bible teacher, opposes this discipling or shepherding theology. He says that once locked into their leadership, 'You cannot make any major decision without their prior approval... They seek to exercise complete authority and control over your life... You must submit to the shepherds in all areas of your life that they deem important and necessary. To refuse to do so is to be marked as a rebel.'[13]

Certainly not all shepherding teachers carry their authority this far, and there are varieties of theologies entitled discipling or shepherding that are not abusive; but in numerous cases it has been carried so far as to dictate whom one is to marry, how much and when one is to give, what one is to read or if one should or should not move away for a job elsewhere. It sounds absurd for anyone to get pulled into a teaching like this, yet when divine authority is claimed, and claimed to be backed by the scriptures, many people become unbelievably docile and allow themselves to be lured into the security the cult offers.

---

13 Chuck Smith, 'Shepherding or Dictatorship?', *The Answer for Today*, The Word for Today, California: p.2

It is not so absurd when we realise that the seduced person, even through the aberrant group, may have had a genuine 'spiritual experience' such as being 'born again'. The group has helped him find God, so how in his mind could the group or its leaders be wrong? How heart-breaking it is that truth is often mingled with a lie, that good is sometimes only a tool for evil or that it is simply misused by those who are deceived, yet sincere. Too often we legitimise our beliefs and our groups' beliefs with our subjective experiences. Our individual experience, group experiences or leaders' experiences often become our proof of being right and in the truth.

Teachers of abusive doctrines place a heavy emphasis on authority by claiming such verses as 'obey your leaders and submit to them' (Hebrews 13:17, NAS) and 'do not touch my anointed ones' (1 Chronicles 16:22, NAS). Cutting right across the grain of such cultic authority and control, the apostle Peter appeals to, but does not command or order, other elders, and thus himself, to 'serve as overseers,' not to be 'lording it over those entrusted to you, but being examples to the flock' (1 Peter 5:2-3, NIV).

The Greek word for 'lords over' means to 'control, exercise dominion over, act as a supreme authority over or subjugate'. The scripture expressly forbids leaders controlling the lives of followers. The same passage does advise the younger persons to submit themselves to the elders; yet even this statement is qualified in this way: 'clothe yourselves with humility towards one another' (1 Peter 5:5, NAS).

Again Smith states, 'Don't try to bring them into submission or subjugation to you.'[14] A demanding husband can require his wife to submit to him. She may obey, but she will be a psychologically and spiritually battered person. He may gain an obedient wife, but he will not have a whole wife. He may think he is leading when he is actually driving or putting her in subjection to him. True submission is not an act: it is a trusting attitude which affects our actions.

In Matthew 20:25-27 we see Jesus commanding his followers not to be like the rulers of this world who exercise dominion

---

14 Chuck Smith, 'Submission', *Answers*, Maranatha Evangelical Association, California: Issue 8, p.4

over others. When group leaders assume rank and power like those of kings and the military, and exercise far-reaching control and authority over their followers, they are in direct conflict with these clear passages in 1 Peter and Matthew.

In the beginning of his second letter to the Corinthians, Paul wrote, 'Not that we lord it over your faith, but we work with you for your joy, because it is by faith you stand firm' (2 Corinthians 1:24, NIV). Paul did not have authority over other people's faith and he did not attempt to gain it. Our personal faith in God is not to be tainted by the demands of others. Paul also wrote to Philemon, 'Therefore, although in Christ I could be bold and order you to do what you ought to do, yet I appeal to you on the basis of love' (Philemon 8-9, NIV). Paul knew he could take advantage of Philemon and misuse his authority; instead he maintained a balanced perspective. A convert of Paul's ministry, Philemon might have taken such a heavy-handed order, but fortunately his pastor was a true leader.

Some discipleship teachers express the need to control disciples while describing a disciple as one who obeys commands. Yet a disciple is one who learns from a master or a holy man, like Jesus, and who lives out his master's godly qualities, not by constraint, but by his own free will and choosing. Christians are called to be disciples of Christ – not disciples of other Christians.

Authoritarian leaders often hide behind an overuse of 'authority scriptures' because of personal fear and an ignorance of their own susceptibility to the allurements of power. While possessing power over others, they lack a perceptive and objective understanding of the scriptures they themselves use to authorise their position. Their interpretation of the oft-touted 'touch not God's anointed' verses is in contradiction to the general pattern of scripture. In addition to hiding behind favourite verses of scripture, cultic leaders often are dishonest or biased in their interpretation and implementation of authority scriptures. They are fuelled by a natural desire to protect themselves, their positions and their ministries from correction.

A good leader, however, guides. He never needs to control or demand unthinking loyalty. A true leader need never assert authority to lead. Sincere, honest, and effective leadership gains its own following without using excuses to acquire or keep authority. A good leader nurtures individual growth and non-rebellious autonomy. While instilling a sense of responsibility for others he also helps others to become responsible for their own religious beliefs, creative conclusions, and self-examination.

Finally, for the sake of order, learning, harmony, and the protection of ourselves, laws and authority roles are instituted, with the approval of the scriptures, common sense, and centuries of social living in countless different societies. Yet authority is God-given responsibility, and should be accompanied by a willingness to serve others faithfully within that responsibility. Authority is not something to be taken or demanded by a few; it is an honour and a precious, fragile privilege entrusted by the many who choose freely one person or several people who will serve the many in maintaining a harmonious and productive society.

Christ gives us a fitting rule for the exercise of authority: 'Whosoever will be chief among you, let him be your servant' (Matthew 20:27, KJV). This servant life is not simply a superficial role. Rather it is the true motivation of the leader — he really does want to serve others. Few leaders can claim such pure, single motivation. I certainly have not developed it anywhere near fully in myself, and I have yet to meet a person who has. The pure calling of a leader is high, perhaps out of reach. Yet striving for this servant goal is our only hope of rescuing ourselves from falling off the tightrope of maintaining a harmonious society and plummeting into the abyss of abuse.

The challenge

All things considered, except for the sensationalism the media sells, cultism is a subject that society in general would like to ignore, forget or deny altogether. This is not an exaggerated criticism. Once all the excitement of gory, frightening details has lost its appeal, such reactions of complacency are common. Media overkill on the subject with its lack of depth for seriously educating has contributed to the general lessening of concern. Many persons who are involved in educating the public on cults will confirm that this frustrating laissez-faire attitude towards cultism exists. Meanwhile millions suffer and millions more become more susceptible due to indifference.

I am not advocating that we should mount a vast anti-cult crusade, nor am I suggesting that everyone should be deeply involved in dealing first-hand with today's cult epidemic. Rather, I am concerned that through a general lack of knowledge and caring interest, the prolific successes of cults will continue until the rights and freedoms we all enjoy are endangered, either by cults themselves or by our overreacting with methods to alleviate cultism that are equally abusive.

In just a few short years, and even months after being exposed as abusive and dangerous, various cults have begun to gain varying degrees of acceptance, despite the testimony of thousands of cult escapees. At the same time the public is being lulled to sleep on the issue, and some people have even been moved to support cults. The pattern is becoming all too familiar: contemporary cults, especially those with large sums of money and with Los Angeles and New York public relations firms to sell them, will find their places in the world's religious mainstream. So cults grow and prosper, and thousands more people will be enslaved and abused.

Because of similarities with legitimate Christian groups, aberrant Christian groups make the subject of cultism more difficult for the Christian leader to deal with. It is sometimes an uncomfortable situation. In discussing with me his attempts to expose a growing aberrant group in Seattle, a colleague lamented over his experiences in going to several area churches to inform them of this aberrant church growing in their midst. None of the pastors he approached was interested enough to take action, despite the fact that most of them were losing members to the group's successful proselytising. Some would not believe my colleague's story even with his documentation of his assertions.

Jeanie Mills, a People's Temple defector, explained her futile attempts to get anyone to consider seriously the truth about Jones. She is quoted as saying, 'They were told. They were begged. But nobody cared. All they cared about... was not getting involved... keeping the status quo.'[15]

---

15 Mel White, op.cit., p.183

One minister kindly admonished me to 'just leave cults alone and dwell on the positive.' It is interesting to note that this minister's Bible contains countless passages which deal with exposing false groups: Ephesians 5:11; 1 John 4:1-3; Jeremiah 29:8-9; Philippians 3:2; the letter to the Christians at Galatia. The exposing of the negatives is essential for the survival of the positives. As one philosopher aptly put it, 'The only thing necessary for the triumph of evil is for good men to do nothing.'

Another minister said he would not allow teaching on cultism in his church because such instruction dealt with evil and would negatively affect his congregation. One would think his congregation was mature enough to handle such subject matter since their average age was well over fifty years old. He too would have done well to consider the Bible's admonitions to 'Have nothing to do with the fruitless deeds of darkness, but rather expose them' (Ephesians 5:11, NIV).

History has shown that ignorance is an extremely fertile bed for the affliction of the masses by the few who hunger after power. Apathy is worse than ignorance; it is a conscious decision of the will to do nothing, because of self-interest, the lack of concern for others, or deep feelings of social impotence. One becomes painfully aware that we are all responsible in some way for this cultic explosion. As demonstrated in previous chapters, cults are products of our environment; they are not just a simplistic phenomenon with some evil leader mesmerising a group of deranged individuals. You and I as members of the human race make up the social environment that produces cultic thinking, cultic theology, cultic leaders, and cultic followers.

Furthermore, we don't really want to deal with the cultic phenomenon since cults reveal an uncomfortable part of our darker side. It is a part of our makeup, and this responsibility for it we often wish we could ignore. We find if we are honest with ourselves, that in some way we all desire power, and we all enjoy having power over others; we discover we seek to gain it for ourselves at the expense of others. We are all susceptible to the abuse of power and the wrongs which are exacted on others to get it. The struggle then lies not just in the public arena but in personal awareness; the struggle against cultism is not just a social battle, but also a personal, moral, psychological and spiritual battle.

Cults will not just go away; neither will their abuses. But we as caring neighbours, citizens, educators, social workers, parents, doctors, ministers, bureaucrats and elected officials can do tangible things to eliminate some roots and causes of cultism. Perhaps we will be motivated to specific action to help ourselves, our neighbours and our posterity by considering this list of cult preventatives. It is not exhaustive.

1. We should not be so naive as to assume that people with a religious cause or title can do no evil. We need to evaluate any group carefully before becoming deeply involved in it.
2. We should not think we could never be seduced by a cult. Highly educated, deeply religious, and atheistic people have all been fooled.
3. Educational programmes are needed in schools, churches and in the media, to focus in on roots and causes as well as signs and patterns of cults to enable persons to recognise cultism.
4. We must be keenly aware of man's insecurities, both innate and environmentally produced, and how cults prey upon them. We must understand that most people to some extent are negatively affected by power and praise.
5. Anyone in a position of significant influence must be responsive to pleas of help in order to prevent further tragedies.
6. Parents should be aware that many young people get into cults because of the love given to them by cult adherents and leaders — love many confess they never received at home.
7. Young people especially will seek out spiritual realities; therefore, parents should selectively expose their children to balanced religious groups. Otherwise, once out on their own, young people may be unable to deal with the many spiritual groups that will reach out to them.
8. Churches need to scrutinise themselves, checking for hypocrisy, shallow thinking and indifference. Churches must genuinely reach out to their communities, and also

be aware of tendencies that make the church an exclusive club.

9. All religious groups must emphasise the importance of community responsibility, and members must be encouraged to make their own decisions. Religious entities must clearly be able to distinguish sincere questioning from maliciousness or rebelliousness. Questions should be met with sensitivity, candour and depth.
10. No group should ever assume it has all truth, or that it is more spiritual than everyone else. Cults carry such thinking only a short step further, and give themselves what they believe to be the justification for abuses.

It certainly is allowable and often necessary to nurture, suggestively direct, and guide people's wills and minds; yet it is never allowable to violate an individual's intellect, moral integrity and autonomy. A person cannot truly believe in anyone if she or he is forced or coercively persuaded. Such people are made into robots programmed for responding — not free moral agents thinking, following or worshipping by personal choice. From the beginning of Genesis to the end of Revelation, we see the scriptures not only allow but, by weight of repetition, encourage the free agency of man.

Truth, the pursuit of philosophical or spiritual integrity, with its resulting emphasis on moral integrity, is the key issue here. Whether scientist, atheist, religionist or moralist we should be socially responsible enough to care about truth. Most of us are seekers and desirers of whatever truth our conception of it might be — social, spiritual or scientific. Those who are abused by cults seek truth, but as cult adherents their honourable pursuit of truth is ended or at least limited in scope.

If a person's or a group's purpose is based on truth or the seeking of truth, neither he nor the group should ever have to implement demands for blind faith or blind obedience. Individual creative thinking should be respected and encouraged. If based on truth, a group need not use any questionable tactics to get members or keep them. Truth can draw people to commitment simply on the merit of being truth.

But, either from intellectual shallowness or spiritual lack, coupled with a desire to be bolstered by growing numbers, many religious groups in fear fall prey to using cultic tactics.

Since Jesus Christ is Western civilisation's most prominently referred to source on spiritual truth, we shall view his position on the free will. Jesus boldly, assertively, and in the view of some, narrowly claimed, 'I am . . . the truth' (John 14:6, NAS). Is this a cultic statement of elitism? No. Because Christ never forced or coerced. Instead he gained followers by his loving personality and caring actions as well as by his authority. He appealed to hearts, and in doing so he made bold, assertive statements, but he did not manipulate or control.

It is crucial to see also that Christ's followers continued and grew in numbers even in the absence of his physical presence. It is his truth and Spirit that maintained and still maintains a following, not his awesome personal charisma. Jesus said: 'Because you have seen me, have you believed? Blessed are they who did not see, and yet believed' (John 20:20, NAS). As author Bernard Henri Levy stated, the ideal state, the antithesis of totalitarianism, is a state where 'God reigns only because he does not govern.'[16] In other words, Levy is saying that a kingdom based on Judeo-Christian teaching is the ideal state because no one is physically or psychologically dominating us. Rather, according to Christian revelation, God through his Holy Spirit moves upon the believer and the Bible's leading and guiding in such a way that the free will of man remains free.

Yes, Christ never violated the free will. In fact, he respected man's free will by his use of the word 'if'. For example, '*If* anyone would come after me, he must deny himself and take up his cross and follow me' (Matthew 16:24, NIV). Full dedication to Christ is predicated upon free, uncoerced choosing. The frequent use in scripture of the word 'if' testifies to the necessity of free choice. Christ desired people to follow him on the basis of a critical examination of himself, his words, and his works (John 5:36). He taught men to be followers not

---

16 Lloyd Billingsley, review of Bernard-Henri Levy, *The Testament of God*, in *Christianity Today*, 5 March 1982, p.30

because they were commanded or coerced, but because they chose honestly and intelligently of their own free will.

In fact, Christ did not make it at all easy to remain a true, committed Christian; that is, one like Christ. He made it much more individually difficult to be Christ-like than to be a church member, a church goer or a cult adherent. He understood the necessary ingredients needed for getting love and pure believers — by making love and belief an unforced choice of the free will.

Perhaps it would do us all good, especially those of us with religious persuasions, to examine more seriously Christ's statement, 'If you hold to my teaching, you are really my disciples. Then you will know the truth, and the truth will set you free' (John 8:32, NIV). All men may then be able to live individually, honourably and peaceably as free moral persons.

2

A look at ourselves

AND SO, AFTER ALL that has been said about the cultic phenomenon, we might now individually and as members of groups ask ourselves, 'How should we live?'

Self cultism

As we find ourselves in the 'me society', there is a tendency to be non-social, if not anti-social. Many socially conscious people become so disillusioned with their failed attempts to bring about social change and improvement through individual or group efforts that they abandon their social activism for non-social or anti-social isolationism. I experienced this isolationist, non-involvement reaction while I was founding and pastoring a church in the Illinois River Valley in Oregon.

Among the cluster of small communities nestled in that area I ministered primarily to counter-culture people who were remnants of the sixties and seventies hippie movement. Discouraged by their failure to change the system as they viewed it, these people had left the activism scene for the 'back-to-nature-phooey-on-the-rest-of-the- world' scene in the mild climate and unpopulated forests of the Illinois Valley. Their attitudes had swung from intense activism and group involvement to non-involvement.

Non-involvement that stems from feelings of helplessness in trying to change social injustices can easily become non-concern, and it can give rise to an increasing over-preoccupation with self. In fact, non-involvement with others causes us to enter into selfism or (as I see it) self cultism.

Because it is found to be a money-maker, selfism is one of the major advertising strategies of today. Ads in newspapers and billboards or on radio and television continually push us to be chic, macho, cool, hot or whatever form in which we accept self as being number one. As members in the 'me society', we are told we deserve the best from designer jeans to fast foods, from fitness clubs to lipsticks. Meanwhile, people cry from starvation, sink into emotional desperation, and wander through spiritual confusion each day without our needed energies and resources.

Yes, the sociologists are correct in evaluating the seventies as the 'me', 'self' or narcissistic decade. What we become in the eighties now unfolding remains to be seen.

As adherents of the 'me generation', we may think we are not abusing others; but we can still abuse them through neglect – neglect that, as we discussed earlier, can drive people into cults to find the personal-social significance we either consciously or unconsciously withhold from them. In serving ourselves we become selfish persons and turn away from becoming complete, whole, and well-rounded social beings. I have found that a selfish person generally uses and abuses others to make gains for himself; and abuse of others tends to be equal to one's own degree of selfism. The basic cause of selfism is in every human being – the drive to gratify self at the expense, or even the abuse, of others.

One reason why communist propaganda is so successful in defeating what it calls capitalism is that it effectively convinces the teeming, restless and underprivileged masses that it is the selfism of capitalism that deprives them of their fair share either by political or economical abuse. Yet it is interesting that communism as it is practised (that is, by the USSR and other similar nations) abuses the freedom of the individual as much as if not more than capitalism. This is because communism, capitalism or any other socio-economic system has not addressed itself to the basic cause of cultism and its abuses; none has addressed our personal drive to gratify self at the expense of others. However, Christ revealed and provided an answer for self-gratification in his primary teachings. The kingdom of Christ (Christianity) makes the issue of self its first and primary issue.

The Bible's view of self

The Bible gives this selfish state of man a different name: fallen man. Christianity teaches that selfism and its consequent abuse of others for gain to self is intrinsic to our natures. According to this teaching, once man sinned he fell out of full companionship with God and gained the knowledge not only of good, but also of evil. A bent towards selfism, this fallenness finds its realisation in the neglect and abuse of self as a whole person and in the neglect and abuse of others.

As we shall see, Christ declared the primary aspect of his revelation was to provide a means of victory for selfish (fallen) man over selfism — the revelation of salvation. Christ and the Bible emphatically teach us we are to be the opposite of anti-social selfists. Instead we are to be socially responsible and socially active creatures. Christ emphasised repeatedly that the greatest kind of person is a selfless person who lives to serve others; that is, to reveal love through actions.

The apostles started out as basically selfish people. They followed Christ at first for less than pure motives; Judas saw money to be gained; James and John saw power and wanted to be 'the greatest'. Speaking to the indignation the other apostles felt at James and John, whose mother had requested Jesus to set them at the left and right sides of his throne (Matthew 20:20-28), Jesus first replied, 'You know that the rulers of the Gentiles lord it over them, and their high officials exercise authority over them. Not so with you...' (verses 25-26, NIV). He made it clear that greatness in God's view is not to be like the worldly rulers and tyrants of his day who 'exercise dominion'.

We have already found the same word used by Peter ('...not lording it over those entrusted to you...', 1 Peter 5:3, NIV). There, too, it means 'to control, to exercise authority over or subjugate.'

In Matthew, once Christ had clearly established what the greatest is not, he went on to explain what it is: 'Instead, whoever wants to become great among you must be your servant, and whoever wants to be first must be your slave...' (Matthew 20:26-27, NIV). So Christ taught that to put self above or before others is not only a poor way to live, but the wrong way to live. Proper, healthy living for oneself and for others is living to serve others.

In a similar passage Christ says, 'For who is greater, the one who is at the table, or the one who serves? Is it not the one who is at the table? But I am among you as one who serves' (Luke 22:27, NIV). Yet the world teaches that the greatest is the one who is the most majestic, grand or important — the one who is served.

Making a final point in Matthew, Jesus said, 'The Son of Man did not come to be served, but to serve, and to give his life as a ransom for many. . .' (Matthew 20:28, NIV) and he exhorted his followers to imitate his example of selflessness. Christ is the antithesis of self cultism — the opposite of an abusing, neglectful, selfish person by ministering to others.

And here in this last passage we also see the Christian message of salvation from a totally new perspective — the perspective of cultism that we have been discussing; for the Christian teaching on salvation is the very opposite of cultism. Christ ended his dissertation on greatness (selfism) by saying he has come to give his life '. . . as a ransom for many. . .'.

Christ was saying something far deeper than that the greatest selfless act is to die for others. Unless we die while rescuing others from physical injury or death, or perhaps in battle, our deaths can normally be of little lasting or far-reaching advantage to others. But Christ's death was a 'ransom'; that is, his death has a value which purchases something for others. In the context of Matthew chapter 20, it purchases for us an ability to be selfless and, therefore, non-cultic. It is the ransoming aspect of his death that was and is important — it has lasting, eternal value.

An earlier Bible passage has a parallel discussion about what it means to be the greatest. Jesus prefaced his answer to 'who is greatest?' by first stating: 'Unless you change and become like little children, you will never enter the kingdom of heaven. . .' (Matthew 18:3, NIV). Then he added, 'Whoever humbles himself like this child is the greatest in the kingdom of heaven' (verse 5, NIV).

Summarising both the Matthew passages, we see that Christ taught that greatness and true non-selfism or non-cultism are found by being changed, which enables us to 'enter the kingdom of heaven' where humility is to be the prevailing attitude of the citizens. Whether its people are Christians or not, Western civilisation has heard it stated many, many times: the preaching of the Christian concept of salvation is that Christ died for our sins, his death was a ransom for our sins (self cultism), and that we must 'get saved', repent or be changed to become members of Christ's spiritual kingdom. We have heard the phrase 'born again' so many times that its meaning has, perhaps, become unclear.

In order to enter his kingdom Christ explained one must be 'born again' or 'born of the Spirit' (John 3:3 and 5, NIV). Christ declared if we believe in him and his ransoming work, if we are converted, if we turn our lives around and place them in him, then we will mystically and actually have a new spiritual birth by his Spirit which empowers and enables us to serve others while forsaking ourselves; and this birth is just the start to ridding ourselves of selfism.

From infancy a baby must be nourished in order to grow into maturity; so it is with the Christian. In Christ we each have a new start or a new birth that enables us individually to overcome the old life of selfism. Full victory is promised to us further down the road from our birthday. The primary task of every Christian should be to mature into full stature – to become fully like Christ. The more one becomes like Christ the more selfless one should become. Christ said he came to serve. Should our duty be any different?

Perhaps we believe the biblical revelation of self, that it is fallen and subject to all sorts of problems – call them neuroses if you like – because of its condition; perhaps we do not. I am thankful that this is our own decision. No coercion. Which brings me to why I believe following Christ, serving Christ or worshipping Christ is not cultic. Again, Christ never did and does not now force, pressure, coerce or abuse to gain or keep followers. It is always a choice of the free will. People who claim to be followers of Christ may use abuses to gain followers, but that makes their disciples followers of men – not Christ. Over 1,000 'ifs' in the Bible attest to the non-coerciveness of true Christianity and its respect for free will and individual choice (for example, 'If anyone would come after me, he must deny himself and take up his cross daily and follow me' – Luke 9:23).

Christ always refused to be worshipped or given place of prominence as just a man. When men improperly worshipped him he rebuked them, ignored them or turned their worship toward God the Father. Christ was the God-man or God-and-man (as Paul proclaimed, God 'appeared in a body' – 1 Timothy 3:16, NIV). Jesus is not to be worshipped as a man or merely a great man; Christians worship him as he is revealed in his divinity. Without his God-nature or divinity, Christ is no one to be worshipped. Taking on human form, Jesus as God the Son lived on earth to be our example in sacrifice and service to others, by being that sacrifice and doing that service himself. While his sinless death and sinless sacrifice purchased our rights to freedom from selfism and cultism, his ascension into heaven and glorification there attested to his deity and our eventual and complete victory over self.

Finally, in leaving earth and going to the Father, Christ is not physically present to 'lord it over us', to subjugate our wills and abuse us. According to the Christian revelation, Christ sent his Holy Spirit to lead and guide us. He still does so. Lead and guide – not control or force. It is pleasing to learn the Holy Spirit is called the 'Comforter', not the coercer or the enforcer. The Holy Spirit speaks in a still small voice to the inner man rather than dictating loudly or dramatically for control.

While it is possible for a Christian to turn towards cultism, it is not Christianity itself that is cultic or abusive. Abuses depend on those individuals who declare Christ and how they declare him. This is equally true for other philosophies and religions. Our Jewish and Muslim friends, for example, need not be cultic. We may disagree with them in some or all of their teachings, but that does not make them cults according to our basic definition: an elitist group that abuses others. We may see Islam as a false religion, but that does not mean all Muslims are cultists. However, like any religion that includes human beings within its membership, Islam and Judaism can both become cultic depending on how they are taught. Hyper-Zionism could be viewed as cultic, as Khomeini's brand of Islam certainly is. Therefore it is imperative that we examine ourselves when we view and treat others in matters of belief.

Do we have love?

The most frequently used Greek word for love in the Bible, *agape*, means a self-sacrificial love. It is considered the highest form of love, a pure form of selflessness and giving.

When the apostle John wrote, 'For God so loved the world that he gave his only begotten son, that whoever believes in him shall not perish but have eternal life. . .' (John 3:16, NIV) he was saying, 'For God loved the world so selflessly, or self-sacrificially, that he gave. . .' God's love is not inert, but is active; his love is not something found only in words, but in action. A person converted from his old selfish nature to Christ's nature is given the same self-sacrificial love which enables him to be a self-sacrificial lover of God and of others. It is his duty to mature in that love and to express it in words and deeds.

Another striking description of God's love is given in Romans, where the littleness of human love is contrasted with the magnitude of God's selfless love: 'Very rarely will anyone die for a righteous man, though for a good man someone might possibly dare to die. But God demonstrates his own love for us in this: While we were still sinners, Christ died for us' (Romans 5:7-8, NIV). A selfless person is one who has that kind of love in his heart which produces loving attitudes and loving actions, even when they mean inconvenience or loss.

Before I came to Christ and was reborn by his Spirit, I could love others as friends and physical or emotional lovers; but after I met the risen Saviour I could self-sacrificially love those people I would not in my selfism have considered worthy of my love. Without his love 'shed abroad' in my heart – without the reality and actual experiencing of God's Spirit working his love out in me – I could never have endured all the pain, misunderstanding and hurts I have experienced in ministering to others. Christ is the provider of love. Christ got to the root of my selfism. He got to the root of the most basic cause of abuse, and thus the most basic cause of cultism – the selfish heart of man.

Gonzalo Baez-Camargo, one of the most influential evangelical theologians in Mexico, put the problem of man this way:

> The main problem in the world continues to be the unconverted heart as the root of all evil – individual and social. I ask my fellow Christians to part with all these ideas

based on Marxism and historical materialism which make social structures the root of all evil. The structures won't change unless the heart is changed, and changed by God's grace in Christ.[17]

In his first letter to the Christians in Corinth, Paul declares that giving of self to others without this God-love is vain, even to the giving of one's physical life:

> If I speak in the tongues of men and of angels, but have not love, I am only a resounding gong or clanging cymbal. If I have the gift of prophecy and can fathom all mysteries and all knowledge, and if I have a faith that can move mountains, but have not love, I am nothing. If I give all I possess to the poor, and surrender my body to the flames, but have not love, I gain nothing (1 Corinthians 13:1-3, NIV).

Before we take on the spiritual and social responsibilities to which Christianity calls us, we would do well to bear in mind our need for the God-given love that is to empower us; without it we are buoyed up only by the doubtful strength of selfism, and that, we have seen, can be turned towards indifference, neglect, and more active abuses if we are not always on our guard.

The word *gospel* means 'good news'. The good news that Christ brought us was that man individually and as a species could through faith in Christ have a personal relationship with God and be set free from selfism and all its resultant bondages. This is brought out in the following words of Jesus:

> If, as is the case, anyone is desiring to come after me as a follower of mine, let him at once begin to lose sight of himself and his own interests, and let him at once begin to take up his cross, and let him start taking the same road in company with me, and let him continue to do so moment by moment.

---

17 John Maust, 'An Interview with Gonzalo Baez-Camargo, Mexico's Grand Old Man of Evangelism', *Christianity Today*, 5 March 1982, p.30

For whoever wants to save his life will lose it, whoever loses his life for me will find it. What good will it be for a man if he gains the whole world, yet forfeits his soul? (Mark 8:34-36) [18]

If you are thinking that I have climbed down from the lofty heights of objectivity and intellectual analysis of cultism to assert unashamedly and boldly that Christ is the answer to the inherent cause of cultism, and thus man's ruin, you are correct.

But keep in mind that I say the answer is Christ — not religion or religions.

18 Kenneth S. Wuest, *Wuest's Word Studies*, Volume 1, Wm B. Eerdmans Publishing Co., Grand Rapids: 1974, p.171. Used by permission

3

A look at the essence of Christian belief

IN ORDER TO HELP YOU analyse groups, I have used such sociological and psychological factors as the abuse of money, abuse of intimacy, information isolation, social isolation and loss of individuality. I hope you can now distinguish between a cultic group as opposed to one simply different from your personal norm.

The orthodox approach

Up to this point the orthodox analysis of groups has not been adequately discussed. Orthodoxy is the ability of a religious group to line up or agree with the commonly accepted or established tenets of a particular faith – for our purpose, the Christian faith. In Christendom orthodoxy is usually more narrowly defined to mean correct in doctrine as pertaining to such early ecumenical creeds as Nicene, Athanasian and Chalcedon. Harold Brown, Professor of Theology at Trinity Evangelical Divinity School, Deerfield, Illinois, in his book *Heresies*, provides a useful definition of both orthodoxy and heresy: '"Orthodoxy" is derived from two Greek words meaning "right" and "honour". Orthodox faith and orthodox doctrines are those that honour God rightly, something that ought to be desirable and good. In Christian usage, the term "heresy" refers to false doctrine, i.e. one that is simply not true and that is, in addition, so important that those who believe it, whom the church calls heretics, must be considered to have abandoned the faith.'[19]

In abandoning the faith one would in most circumstances be considered lost spiritually and be outside the realm of

---

19 Harold O J. Brown, *Heresies*, Doubleday and Co., Inc., Garden City: 1984, p.1

receiving God's saving grace. There are individual exceptions to this rule: that is, there may be individuals who as members of a heretical group could still have found personal faith in Jesus Christ as saviour. A group or individual that is unorthodox, should they or he continue to become more deviant, will eventually cross from unorthodoxy into heresy.

A system of orthodoxy then is a safeguard for the individual, group, Christendom and the world, but is certainly far from an exact science. Various Christian denominations differ on which ecumenical creeds they may hold to but the differing creeds have a commonality — an orthodoxy. For example in the doctrine of God the Westminster Shorter Catechism does not elaborate on the theology of the Trinity as thoroughly as the Athanasian Creed but they both agree that there are distinctly three persons in the Godhead (Father, Son and Holy Spirit) who are one God — equal in power, glory and substance. What is one Christian's determination of heresy may be another's definition of unorthodoxy while what one considers 'off' or 'suspect' may clearly be unorthodox to the next person. Orthodoxy could be considered the inner-perimeter of safety while the line that divides unorthodoxy from heresy could be seen as the outer line of safety (see Appendix D).

As previously mentioned, at one time Christians determined cultic leanings solely on the basis of their orthodoxy or lack thereof. I noted that while the orthodox method has its value, it also has weaknesses. Some argue with merit that this historical procedure is subjective and can be self-serving. Established groups may conclude that anything new and different is cultic or heretical, which often results in the abuse of others. For example, during the Reformation and Counter-reformation the Catholic church tortured and killed Lutherans and Reformed Christians for their new beliefs such as 'justification by faith and not by works'. Later the followers of Luther and other reformists such as Zwingli drowned or hanged Anabaptists for their new belief that infant baptism was not biblical. In both cases established groups slipped into a self-serving inquisitional mentality.

So the historical or orthodox mode does have potential for abuse. This is not to say the approach is not valid. My studies have resulted in a personal conviction that a majority of groups which deviate from orthodoxy *do* become cultic in the sociological and psychological sense. However, the orthodox church must be careful in the treatment of suspect groups because it is possible that in the early stages of deviation they can be rescued by 'speaking the truth in love' (Ephesians 4:15. See also Galatians 6:1). Open attacks from an orthodox assembly may drive a fledgling suspect group into social and psychological isolation and thus accentuate its 'culticness'.

Also it can work in a converse manner. Because a group has sociological and psychological quirks it can produce unorthodox theology. Which came first, the chicken or the egg? It's often difficult to ascertain if the psychological and sociological abuses produced a lack of orthodoxy or vice versa.

A classic example is a suspect church in Seattle, Washington, USA, known as Community Chapel – a large, thriving pentecostal church in the swirl of controversy for several years. The group is considered a cult by some Christian sources for two primary reasons:

(1) Its unorthodox belief regarding the Trinity. Community Chapel holds to a modified 'Oneness doctrine', a different view of the triunity of God. While their creed professes belief in the Father, Son and Holy Spirit, it pronounces them less separate than traditional trinitarianism. Although Community Chapel professes to be relatively orthodox in some other areas, because of a disparate view of the Godhead it has become isolated by much of the orthodox community. Subsequently, in twenty years Community Chapel has become – according to analysts such as Professor Ronald Enroth – cultic, in the psychological and sociological sense.

(2) Enroth also points to the behaviour, statements and teachings of the chapel's pastor, Donald Barnett, as one of the primary causes of the church's culticness. Barnett holds absolute authority over the church and in his sermons has likened himself to Moses and purports to have visions in which he became one with Jesus and interacted with angels. Members' lives are controlled and manipulated. The group is religiously and socially isolated from the rest of Christendom and the world. More recently Barnett has been teaching a new

'revelation from God' called 'connecting'. He reasons that by having intimate spiritual experiences with members of the opposite sex other than your spouse you can defeat demons of jealousy and find a deepening experience of the love of Christ. Reports from those leaving Community Chapel note that this connecting has simply resulted in sexual promiscuity, broken marriages and broken homes.

Whether the church is a full-blown cult or not has been debated for some time. If it isn't a cult in the fullest sense it surely is on the road to becoming so. Ten years ago the church was basically a legitimate holiness, pentecostal church. The deviations have been part of a long subtle process not intentionally deviant. Deception is not usually intentional but the result of something deeply wrong. Ten years ago deviant theologies such as an almost total preoccupation with demons and connecting would never have been tolerated at Community Chapel.

Some people believe the aberrations at Community Chapel began with basic insecurities in Barnett — a man who couldn't handle power. Power often increases one's vulnerability and fears which result in a need for more power which results in more fear and on and on goes the mad spiral of megalomania, amplified by Barnett's high view of himself as God's man for the hour. A nineteen-seventies trend in conservative Christian circles of emphasising the authority of Christian leaders and total submission of believers to leaders certainly didn't help check Barnett's increasing power base and demands of unbending loyalty. As the Chapel's aberrations grew and became more apparent so did criticism from without and within the organisation; the criticism being counteracted by Barnett with an exercising of more authority and power and greater demand of total submission.

Others believe the aberrations resulted from and grew from what most of Christendom believes to be the Chapel's unorthodox view of the Godhead.

Whether the Chapel is or becomes a full-blown cult or whether it is rescued from its spiral into deepening culticness will depend upon the actions and teachings of Barnett as well as the reactions and treatment the Chapel and its individual adherents receive from the Christian community at large. The chicken and egg debate comes clearly into play. What has been causing the Chapel's deviant direction: its lack of orthodoxy, or its social isolation, exclusiveness and the pride of its leader and members? It's very probable the answer is that both causes have interplayed to produce its culticness. The causes can be quite different for different suspect groups. The point is that sensitivity and careful analysis must be used by orthodox groups in evaluating suspect groups.

Another religion's differing views or non-orthodoxy do not necessarily make it a cult in the abusive sense but do make it a different religion – in other words, an aberration or non-Christian. It is here we find disagreement among Christian cult experts and Christian theologians. Some experts believe if a group is non-orthodox in areas such as the Godhead or Trinity then members of such groups cannot be 'saved', that is, be recipients of the saving knowledge and grace of Jesus Christ. Others conversely believe that groups such as Community Chapel that hold to a non-orthodox trinitarian point of view may be 'off' but individual members can still be saved if they have expressed personal faith in Christ as Saviour and Lord. I agree. I believe it was Francis Schaeffer, the acclaimed twentieth-century philosopher and theologian, who in one of his books noted that some of church history's most sincere Christians were heretics. Deceived people may be unchristian in the orthodox sense but Christian in the spiritual sense of a personal relationship with God through Christ. An in-depth look at Jim Jones and Peoples' Temple reveals great deception but many had a personal relationship with Christ.

Even within groups that have similar unorthodox beliefs there are differing degrees of deviation, necessitating an even more refined mode of evaluating religious organisations. For instance, the United Pentecostal Churches (UPC) teach a 'oneness' doctrine similar to Community Chapel and are thus unorthodox but are not usually considered a cult as is Community Chapel. UPC groups are separatists (seeing themselves as unique) due to such aberrations as the belief that salvation is only possible for those who speak in tongues, but are not considered heretical to the point of being lost spiritually. Many UPC churches and adherents are considered by various orthodox churches as certainly different but fellow

Christians. Community Chapel would probably be in the same class as UPC churches (deviant rather than a cult) if its other previously-mentioned theological, sociological and psychological aberrations brought on by Barnett were absent. If the Chapel and the UPC were to simply deny the full deity of Christ, which Jehovah's Witnesses do, then they would be much more obviously heretical.

I believe that very often, where unorthodoxy reaches the heretical stage, such as amongst Jehovah's Witnesses, who deny the full deity of Christ, adherents cannot be saved because they actually believe in a different Christ. They believe in a Christ who is not biblical or Christian in the classical sense.

A closer look at unorthodox Christian groups who have not yet crossed the line into full heresy will reveal they are frequently recipients of salvation through faith in Christ. Pastors from several respected denominations who have taken a closer look at Community Chapel have found this to be true. These pastors used a sensitive, more discerning approach and in having fellowship with Chapel members have come to honour Chapel members as being 'saved' brothers and sisters in Christ. Certain observers hold they cannot be Christians since they have an unorthodox theology. I disagree as do others. Dr Eldred Nelson and his assistant pastor, George Page, of a Seattle Assembly of God church, after examining Barnett's teachings on the Godhead and talking with Chapel members and ex-members, suspect the Chapel's theological position on the Trinity is not so much deviant as semantic. Dr Nelson contends Barnett is using the issues of his 'special revelations' such as his teaching on the Godhead as a tool to keep followers. In dialoguing with ex-Chapel members he has found them to be clearly recipients of Christ's saving grace.

Dr Nelson's example of close and careful examination and evaluation is in much need to be copied throughout the Christian world. When asked why they didn't leave People's Temple when things went so bad survivors uniformly replied, 'Where could we go?' In other words, 'Who would accept us? Where could we go to be cared for and protected? Who could we trust?' Dr Nelson's church has become that outlet for those leaving Community Chapel. His open heart and that of

Assistant Pastor George Page have created a haven for ex-Chapel followers. Thank God they have some place to go before a potential Jonestown tragedy occurs.

The Assemblies of God denomination in general is also an admirable example of sensitivity and care. The Assemblies of God split earlier in this century over the trinitarian-oneness controversy, yet despite old wounds, Northwest Assembly of God Bible College Professor Dr Daniel Pecota, while criticising Barnett's aberrations, extended the hand of help and fellowship to Chapelites.

While many cultic groups are non-trinitarian it is not impossible for members of non-trinitarian groups to be Christians. Despite Mormonism's aberrations in their teachings on the nature of God and Christ, I personally know Mormons who have a relationship with Christ but who are still ignorantly involved with unorthodox doctrines.

While most Christians including myself disassociate themselves from organisations such as Community Chapel we must (and I do) extend the hand of fellowship to any individual who professes a clear, unmistakable commitment to Jesus Christ as Saviour and Lord despite their aberrations. Usually attacking alone does not help rescue people from cults. Very infrequently is a loving hand of care and compassion extended to draw people out. Pastors in Seattle should be commended for doing both: exposing the wrongs and evils while extending the hand of fellowship to draw, heal, nurture and guide back into mainstream Christendom.

Groups like Community Chapel point to the fact there are no hard, fast, orthodox theological rules which can always be applied in the same manner to all organisations. Today's religious potpourri is far too complicated and diverse. As demonstrated, there can be exceptions to the rule as far as non-orthodox groups having Christians in their membership. All-encompassing rules or orthodoxy can't always apply in every case.

However, it is essential for the Christian to understand the historical, foundational doctrines of the Christian faith in order to wade through the modern maze of religious beliefs and to discern which groups are Christian, deviant, non-Christian or cultic. For the Christian to properly and fully retain the title 'Christian' requires a determination of what it is a Christian does or does not believe.

Therefore, while on one hand we recognise that a group's orthodoxy doesn't guarantee it being non-cultic in the abusive sense and that non-orthodoxy doesn't always mean individuals are denied the saving grace of Jesus Christ, the orthodox analysis method, despite its potential for abuse and its imperfections, is a fundamental and necessary tool. Without it we have no standards. Without it we must discount the wisdom of thousands of Christian leaders and theologians including church fathers and those of the famous church councils. Without a system or standard of orthodoxy which includes man-made doctrinal statements, we will wander in a wilderness of uncertainty, confusion and consequently become 'lost', either temporarily or permanently, partially or completely. Christendom's system of orthodoxy with its creeds takes a lot of guesswork out of our spiritual journey in this life and helps prepare us for the next life. This doesn't mean we should be afraid to examine our creeds for they are man-made and subject therefore to scrutiny. Besides, the rise of cultism will bring orthodoxy to the test anyway. Keep in mind we have examples in church history that some of those who brought orthodoxy to the test had something good to teach Christendom. Where would the truths of baptism by immersion and justification by faith be without the challenges to established beliefs brought by Luther, Zwingli and the Anabaptists? We must be thankful to our church forefathers whose councils, debates and challenges have protected and nourished the Christian faith.

To be a Christian in the truest sense it is necessary to be true to the word Christian; to be true to Christ and the Bible and its truths as they were 'once delivered to the saints' (Jude 3, NAS) by Jesus (2 John 1:9) and the apostles (Acts 2:42). It would be illogical for a Muslim to say he was a part of Islam but did not believe in Mohammed as 'the true prophet'. It is logical then for a person, if he claims to be a Christian, to carefully follow Christ, his teachings, the Bible and the truths delivered by the New Testament apostles and prophets. A Christian who uses this logic would then be orthodox.

Let us now pursue the basics of Christian orthodoxy.

Following Christ

Important orthodox indicators of whether a group is Christian or not are: whether it follows Christ and his teaching and the manner in which it follows him. Jesus emphatically stated, 'I am the way, the truth and the life and no one comes to the Father but through me. . . if a man comes to God through any other means he is a thief and a robber' (John 14:6; 10:8, NAS). Christ made many such statements.

Christian author and philosopher, C.S. Lewis, aptly said that Jesus either told the truth, was a liar or mentally deranged. There are no other options.

Given the life of Christ, his miracles, his teachings, his character, his death and resurrection, his fulfilment of over three hundred Old Testament prophecies, and given the historical, archaeological and logical proofs of the authenticity and divine inspiration of the Bible, one finds it difficult intellectually to come to the conclusion that Christ was a liar or a lunatic. One is left with the alternative that Jesus is who he said he was, that he told the truth in all matters and that he gave us divine truth.

As to remaining doctrinally orthodox, John the apostle cautions: 'Anyone who goes too far and does not abide in the teaching of Christ does not have God; the one who abides in the teaching has both the Father and the Son. If anyone comes to you and does not bring this teaching, do not receive him into your house, and do not give him a greeting; for the one who gives him a greeting participates in his evil deeds' (2 John 9-11, NAS).

Jesus advised his followers many times to beware of false prophets and false christs. Such a passage is the following: 'For many will come in my name, saying "I am the Christ," and will mislead many. Then if anyone says to you, "Behold, here is the Christ," or "There he is," do not believe him. For false christs and false prophets will arise and will show great signs and wonders, so as to mislead, if possible, even the elect. Behold, I have told you in advance' (Matthew 24:5, 23-25, NAS). Followers of Rev. Sung Myung Moon (Moonies) of the Unification Church Association believe Rev. Moon to be the Lord of the Second Coming while the Jehovah's Witnesses teach Christ returned invisibly to the earth in 1914. It seems Matthew 24 has been overlooked.

The apostle Paul wrote, 'I am amazed you are so quickly deserting him who called you by the grace of Christ, for a different gospel... But even though we, or an angel from heaven, should preach to you a gospel contrary to that which we have preached to you, let him be accursed' (Galatians 1:6,8 NAS). The Mormons teach an angel presented a different gospel to the Mormon founder, Joseph Smith. This new revelation from the Angel Moroni, supposedly written on golden tablets, became *The Book of Mormon*. In addition to 'translating' *The Book of Mormon*, Smith 'revised' sections of the King James Bible and wrote additional 'revelations' compiled in the *Pearl of Great Price*. *The Book of Mormon* and the *Pearl of Great Price* along with another 'sacred' writing by Joseph Smith entitled *Doctrine and Covenants* are revered as much if not more than the Bible.

In numerous passages the Bible speaks of what is false or non-Christian doctrine. In 1 Timothy 4:1-3 we read: 'But the Spirit explicitly says that in the later times some will fall away from the faith, paying attention to deceitful spirits and doctrines of demons, by means of hypocrisy of liars seared in their own conscience as with a branding iron, men who forbid marriage, advocate abstaining from foods...' (NAS).

In 2 Timothy 3:1-8 we read:

> But realise this, that in the last days difficult times will come. For men will be lovers of self, lovers of money, boastful, arrogant, revilers, disobedient to parents, ungrateful, unholy, unloving, irreconcilable, malicious gossips, without self-control, brutal, haters of good, treacherous, reckless, conceited, lovers of pleasure rather than lovers of God; holding to a form of godliness, although they have denied its power; and avoid such men as these. For among them are those who enter into households and captivate weak women weighed down with sins, led on by various impulses, always learning and never able to come to the knowledge of the truth. And just as Jannes and Jambres opposed Moses, so these men also oppose the truth, men of depraved mind, rejected as regards the faith (NAS).

For the Christian it is crucial to determine if he or she follows 'the faith' or just any faith; it is also crucial to know if he or she follows someone else who doesn't follow 'the faith'.

Few religious groups could better fit the criteria laid down in these Bible passages than the Rajneesh group which, until November 1985, was centred in Antelope, Oregon, USA. Rajneesh also has a large following in Europe and a beachhead in the Hillman, Western Australia, area. Religious leaders and government and law enforcement officials in the state of Oregon involved in investigations and indictments of the Rajneesh leadership brought forth evidence that suggests the group could be a fulfilment of 1 and 2 Timothy: 'lovers of money, boastful, arrogant, unloving, irreconcilable, malicious, treacherous, conceited and lovers of pleasure rather than lovers of God.' Sheela, Bhagwan Shree Rajneesh's former fiery lieutenant, has been charged with several felonies. The Bhagwan agreed to leave the US due to charges brought against him.

In Christ's dissertation on his second coming as recorded in Matthew chapter 24, he warns of an unparalleled growth in false religions and leaders, noting the time will be like the 'days of Noah' when men were obsessed with 'eating and drinking and giving in marriage.' 'Party time' is the philosophy of many modern-day cults and non-Christian religions such as the Rajneesh group. 'Eat, drink and be merry for tomorrow we die...', as the ancient Greeks taught, is nothing but old-fashioned Epicureanism – sin and self-indulgent pleasure carried to the extreme.

Who is the Christian and the world following? The Christ of the Bible, or the false christs and teachers the Bible repeatedly admonishes us to avoid?

Unity in diversity

Within Christendom there are varied interpretations of theology and church doctrines. How can we determine which is deviant, cultic or heretical? Is there common theological ground defining what is orthodox? Yes!

Christendom is pluralistic, made up of diverse groups with diverse opinions and theological positions. Some think this is Christianity's great flaw. Not so. The Bible declares we

Christians will all one day be of one faith but in the meantime we are exhorted to 'endeavour to keep the unity of the Spirit' (Ephesians 4:3, KJV).

Diversity, exemplified in creation and pre-eminently in human nature, can be beautiful and beneficial, if love and mutual respect are its bonds. Jesus knew that his church would have individual differences and cautioned us to forbear and forgive one another. He taught that where dissimilar views existed, Christian love and respect would convince the world of true allegiance to him: 'A new commandment I give to you, that you love one another. By this all men will know that you are my disciples, if you have love for one another' (John 13:34-35, NAS).

So Christians are heterogeneous but grouped within commonly accepted biblical tenets delivered by Christ and the apostles as revealed in scripture, such as: the atoning work of Christ on the cross, the resurrection of Christ, the second coming of Christ, and the divine inspiration of the Bible, among others.

For the sake of simplicity, retention and practical application, in order to avoid doctrinal hairsplitting, we will examine the most basic areas of Christian orthodoxy and see how they compare with the beliefs of other religious groups and movements. Christianity's four basic questions are: 'Who is Jesus Christ?'; 'Who is God?'; 'Who is man?'; and, 'What are the requirements for salvation or eternal life?'.

Who is Jesus Christ?

The apostle John in the waning years of his life gave guidelines to ascertain who is and who is not a Christian. 1 John 4:1-6 reads:

> Beloved, do not believe every spirit, but test the spirits to see whether they are from God; because many false prophets have gone out into the world. By this you know the Spirit of God: every spirit that confesses that Jesus Christ has come in the flesh is from God; and every spirit that does not confess Jesus is not from God; and this is the spirit of the antichrist, of which you have heard that it is coming, and now it is already in the world. You are from God, little child-

ren, and have overcome them; because greater is he who is in you than he who is in the world. They are from the world; therefore they speak as from the world, and the world listens to them. We are from God; he who knows God listens to us; he who is not from God does not isten to us. By this we know the spirit of truth and the spirit of error (NAS).

John declares the 'spirit of error' is indicated by any doctrine excluding the humanity or divinity of Christ.

John 1:1 and 14 confirms this: 'In the beginning was the Word, and the Word was with God, and the Word was God. And the Word became flesh and dwelt among us, and we beheld his glory, glory as of the only begotten from the Father, full of grace and truth' (NAS).

In Colossians 2:9 we read, 'For in him all the fullness of deity dwells in bodily form' (NAS). The apostle Paul in Ephesians 1:23 describes Jesus as 'the fullness of him who fills all in all.'

Can a person be both man and God? The Bible tells us how it happened: 'Now the birth of Jesus Christ was as follows. When his mother Mary had been betrothed to Joseph, before they came together she was found to be with child by the Holy Spirit' (Matthew 1:18, NAS). 'And the angel answered and said to her, "The Holy Spirit will come upon you, and the power of the Most High will overshadow you; and for that reason the holy offspring shall be called the Son of God" ' (Luke 1:35 NAS).

Jesus' own statements indicate that he saw himself as having full humanity and full deity. He said, '. . . you shall die in your sins; for unless you believe that I am He, you shall die in your sins' (John 8:24, NAS). According to Greek scholars, the phrase 'I am He', *ego eimi*, is the Greek form of the Old Testament name of God, the great I Am, or Jehovah, meaning that Jesus claimed to be *the Timeless One*. In John 8:58, as well, Jesus states he is the Jehovah of the Old Testament, not just 'a god', as Jehovah's Witnesses teach, from using their poor translation of John 1:1. Jesus declared he and his Father 'are one' (John 10:30, 17:11,22).

Jesus as man hungered, ate, became fatigued, and died. As God he was worshipped, declared equal and one with God the Father and raised his own human body from the dead. 'I have the authority to lay [my life] down, and I have the authority to take it again' (John 10:18 NAS). In John 2:19-21, Jesus said, 'Destroy this temple and in three days I will raise it up' (NAS).

Jehovah's Witnesses are not the only ones in direct disagreement with the Christian tenet that Jesus Christ is fully God and fully man. Other groups have their own individual aberrations. Mormons teach Jesus is the spirit brother of Lucifer (the devil), one of many gods. Worldwide Church of God or Armstrongism denies that Jesus is equal to the Father. Baha'i contends that Christ is not God, but a 'manifestation' like Baha'u'llah. Christian Science, Hinduism, Buddhism, Islam, Hare Krishna, Transcendental Meditation and the nation of Islam (formerly Black Muslims) contradict the historical Christian position.

Who is God?

Biblical Christian theology teaches that God is a Person. He is neither some impersonal force in the universe nor is he human, though in Jesus Christ he took on humanity in order to relate to us through his sacrificial death. He is Creator. There are no other gods beside him, he being the one and only God who reveals himself as Father, Son and Holy Spirit. Christian orthodoxy acknowledges God to be beyond what human thought can entirely capture. For example, he is omniscient (all knowing) and omnipresent (present everywhere). He is Spirit. He is eternal.

In contrast the Hindus view God (Brahma) as being without form, abstract and eternal: without attributes, therefore: not a person. Hare Krishna adherents also are convinced of many lesser gods while avowing there is one supreme God. Mormons likewise insist there are many gods, that God is a material being once human, that humans may achieve godhood through works. Similarly, the Worldwide Church of God teaches that men can become gods. Transcendental Meditation's view is that there is no difference between God and creation. Buddhism and Christian Science deny God as a personal deity.

The Unification Church Association (Moonies) teaches, as do many religious movements, that there is no triune expression of God. Unitarians deny the doctrine of the Trinity saying the Father is a Principle of Mind, not a person. The Worldwide Church of God also denies the Trinity, noting that God is a family and a kingdom and that we can become gods.

Repeatedly, the Bible refers to God using personal pronouns, meaning God is a person. Look at the following example: 'For God so loved the world that he gave his only begotten Son, that whosoever believes in him should not perish, but have eternal life' (John 3:16, NAS). God is characterised as a Creator and a person in this passage: 'In the beginning God created the heavens and the earth . . . and God created man in his own image, in the image of God he created him, male and female he created them' (Genesis 1: 1, 27, NAS).

God's oneness yet plurality as Father, Son and Holy Spirit or trinity is seen in the following: 'Let us make man in our image, according to our likeness . . .' (Genesis 1:26, NAS). The scene at the water baptism of Jesus demonstrates the existence and interaction of the Father, Son and Holy Spirit: 'And after being baptised, Jesus went up immediately from the water; and behold, the heavens were opened, and he saw the Spirit of God descending as a dove, and coming upon him, and behold, a voice out of the heavens, saying, "This is my beloved Son, in whom I am well pleased" ' (Matthew 3:16,17, NAS).

At the close of Matthew's gospel we see God as expressed through the trinity: 'Go therefore and make disciples of all the nations, baptising them in the name of the Father, Son and Holy Spirit' (Matthew 28:19, NAS).

In a perusal of 1 John 5:6-13, we observe a reference to Jesus Christ the Son of God, the Holy Spirit and God as the Father of Jesus Christ.

Who is man?

The Bible discloses that man was created in the 'image and likeness' of God (Genesis 1:26,27, NAS); that man was the pinnacle of God's creation, designed to think and act like God yet not God himself. Man fell out of fellowship with God through disobedience and thereby lost full dominion over creation (Genesis 3), lost being fully in the likeness of God, lost the full favour of God.

The scriptures inform us that since Adam every man and

woman has sinned (Romans 3:10-12; Ephesians 2:3; Psalm 51:5; Jeremiah 17:9) except for 'Jesus Christ the righteous' (1 John 2:1, NAS). This important distinction of Christ's sinlessness and man's sinfulness is affirmed in Hebrews 4:14-16 (LB): '. . . Jesus the Son of God . . . understands our weaknesses, since he had the same temptations we do, though he never once gave way to them and sinned.' Romans 3:23 declares: 'For all have sinned and fall short of the glory of God' (NAS). Romans 3:24,25 goes on to say we are redeemed from our sinful state by God's gift of love through faith in the sacrificial work of Jesus Christ that we might be 'justified', or declared not guilty.

The Bible states that man's basic nature is inclined towards evil or sinful, also asserting man can *never* become God. He can become a child of God but never equal with God (Isaiah 43:10; 44:6,8; Hosea 11:9; Numbers 23:19). Furthermore man cannot save himself through his own effort (Ephesians 2:8,9; Titus 3:5; Galatians 2:16; Isaiah 64:6).

Nearly all cults and world religions contradict biblical Christian principles as to who man is in relation to God. Hinduism asserts every man is God; Buddhism avows man can save himself; The Moonies state that man's own works can save him; the nation of Islam (formerly Black Muslims) asserts that white men are by nature evil but black men are good and divine; Transcendental Meditation preaches that man can find God if he looks within himself; and the Worldwide Church of God emphasises humans are able to become gods.

The greatest deception today is the belief being pushed by the human potential movement and Hindu-influenced cults and aberrant Christian groups that man is potentially, if not actually, a god, or God.

In Ephesians 2 (LB), there is a beautiful summary of who God is, who man is and how the gift of God in the work of Jesus Christ saves us by faith, making us not God, or gods, but temples or dwelling places for God's Spirit:

> Because of his kindness you have been saved through trusting in Christ. And even trusting is not of ourselves; it too is a gift from God. Salvation is not a reward for the good we have done, so none of us can take any credit for it. It is

God himself who has made us what we are and given us new lives from Christ Jesus...

But now you belong to Christ Jesus, and though you once were far away from God, now you have been brought very near to him because of what Jesus Christ has done for you with his blood.

Now all of us, whether Jews or Gentiles, may come to God the Father with the Holy Spirit's help because of what Christ has done for us.

We who believe are carefully joined together with Christ as parts of a beautiful, constantly growing temple for God. And you also are joined with him and with each other by the Spirit, and a part of this dwelling place of God.

Eternal life — salvation

Our discussion of 'Who is man?' brings us to the topic of eternal life, or salvation. We've noted that various religions declare that man earns his own way to eternal life and/or becomes God. The Bible repudiates such deception by teaching we are saved by grace (undeserved, unearned favour from God) through faith in Christ and his atoning sacrifice on the cross, salvation being a gift of God, not something earned by our good deeds.

Romans 10:9 explains salvation this way: 'If you confess with your mouth Jesus as Lord, and believe in your heart that God raised him from the dead, you shall be saved; for with the heart man believes, resulting in righteousness, and with the mouth he confesses, resulting in salvation' (NAS).

The Bible loudly announces that all humans have fallen from the state of eternal life by sinning (Romans 3:10-12; 3:23; 6:23) and that sin is the breaking of God's laws (1 John 3:4). Hinduism on the other hand teaches there is no absolute good or evil and if a person is unable to save himself in this life span through devotion, meditation and good works he gets another chance at salvation in one or more future incarnations.

The Bible reveals that man lives and dies on this earth once, and then comes the judgment (Hebrews 9:27). In other words, we get one chance at life and eternal life, with no future reincarnated chances. Thank God our salvation isn't based upon what we do or do not do but upon who Jesus is and what he did. Our performance vacillates but Jesus and what he did 'is the same yesterday and today, yes and forever' (Hebrews 13:8, NAS).

Since most non-Christian religions have a works ethic formula for man to save himself and often ignore absolutes of right and wrong, here is the problem: If man is told he has no sin and there are no absolutes, then man is not responsible for his actions, whether good or evil.

Such is the view of Rajneesh and his Orange People who basically believe in hedonism or self-indulgent pursuit of pleasure regardless of how it may affect others. Consequently, a man convinced he has no sin or responsibility for his actions has no need of a Saviour – especially if he thinks he can get another chance at earning enough points to make it in the next life. Therefore we have a rejection of Christ as he revealed himself. It must be concluded if we are not in sin, he died in vain as a sinless sacrifice for mankind.

Such beliefs bring man to a state of social irresponsibility. 'What do I care if my sin or my actions affect another person? There is no right or wrong. The only important thing is that it was pleasurable for me.'

For other religions to state they believe in and follow Christ while proclaiming there are various ways to salvation including other prophets or teachers at best exposes ignorance of Christ's claims or at worst unmasks hypocrisy or dishonesty. How so? Ignorance is involved because Christ left no option for eternal life except in himself; dishonesty enters in because such people take what appeals to them from Christ's teachings but ignore Christ's claim to be the only way to eternal life.

John 14:6 records Jesus as saying, 'I am the way, and the truth, and the life; no one comes to the Father but through me' (NAS). In the Greek language from which this passage was translated, 'the' is before the words 'way', 'truth' and 'life' and means 'entirely or exclusively'. Jesus said anyone else claiming to be the way is 'a thief and a robber' (John 10:1, NAS). So according to Jesus you cannot follow others and hope to be on the right track. He left no middle ground. Biblically speaking, Jesus cannot be a part of our bag of beliefs or one of our saviours. Such a position is incongruous with his teaching. If we do not wholly accept him and him only then we reject him. 'He who is not with me is against me; and he who does not gather with me scatters' (Matthew 12:30, NAS).

To become and remain a Christian requires complete and sole commitment to Jesus Christ. Hinduism has experienced a great revival in its various forms in Western society despite the fact that its persuasions – a caste system, animals believed to be reincarnated humans – have reduced the masses in India to abject poverty, hunger and a state of suppressive discrimination. The Academy Award-winning movie *Gandhi* recently added to this deceased Indian leader's popularity and to Western fascination with Hinduism. In the midst of it all, many non-Christians and some Christians have concluded that Gandhi was a Christian, even a Messiah, or Christ himself.

Mohandas K. Gandhi was a great man and a leader to be admired, but not Christ; nor did he claim to be. Neither was he 'saved' in the Christian sense of the word. Many assume his salvation because of his good works (and great works he did do) but the Bible does not impart salvation based upon works but upon Jesus Christ and what he did on the cross for us. Out of a work of God in our hearts through Jesus Christ, good works should flow from us to others.

Gandhi stated he could not believe that Jesus Christ was the only incarnate Son of God, or that belief in him was the only way to everlasting life. Gandhi could not confess Christ as Lord. Hear what Jesus had to say about Gandhi's conclusions: 'And he summoned the multitude with his disciples, and said to them, "If anyone wishes to come after me, let him deny himself, and take up his cross, and follow me. For whoever wishes to save his life shall lose it; but whoever loses his life for my sake and the gospel's shall save it. For what does it profit a man to gain the whole world, and forfeit his soul? For whoever is ashamed of me and my words in this adulterous and sinful generation, the Son of Man will also be ashamed of him when he comes in the glory of his Father with the holy angels' (Mark 8:34-38, NAS).

> Everyone therefore who shall confess me before men, I will also confess them before my Father who is in heaven. But

> whoever shall deny me before men, I will also deny him before my Father who is in heaven. Do not think that I came to bring peace on the earth; I did not come to bring peace, but a sword . . . and he who does not take his cross and follow after me is not worthy of me. He who has found his life shall lose it, and he who has lost his life for my sake shall find it. He who receives you receives me, and he who receives me receives him who sent me (Matthew 10:32-40, NAS).

It narrows down to this: What have you done with Jesus? What has mankind done with Jesus? Will men recognise that they require a saviour, a redeemer, a pure sacrifice for sin to satisfy God's justice? Will you?

Liar, lunatic or Lord of all?

For the Christian – according to Christ's own word – there can be no in-between, no alternatives. Full acceptance or total rejection. An awesome decision.

But the choice is ours. No coercion. Just an invitation to examine Christ and his word to decide for ourselves.

Let 'God be found true, though every man be found a liar' (Romans 3:4, NAS).

4

A look at some religious movements

CULTISM CONTINUES to grow in magnitude and diversity, creating a complex phenomenon difficult to analyse and impossible to fully counter.

This is a brief review of various religions, splinter groups and cults in order to give at least a rudimentary feel for our world's religious potpourri. Bear the following in mind as you read this review:

First, the reader has an opportunity to apply all that has been so far discussed: if a Christian, to apply the test of orthodoxy; and if a Christian or non-Christian, to apply the sociological and psychological determinants.

Second, the reader can use intelligent discernment. I have found that most people would just like a simplistic black and white list of groups in two categories: good and bad. While such lists have merit in other works, this book is dedicated to educating and equipping everyday people and professionals with their own critical acumen. Because non-orthodox and cultic groups are far too many to list and because the variety and proliferation in number and size of such groups are too vast to keep up with, I find it better to develop acuity rather than lists. This makes for greater sensitivity, respect and for a healthier religious environment.

Third, bear in mind when applying critical acumen that our basic definition declares a cult to be an elitist group that abuses others. A Christian cult group is one that abuses and/or is grossly deviant from Christian orthodoxy.

Fourth, such groups as Islam and Judaism, Hinduism and Buddhism are definitely other religions and far from Christian orthodoxy but that does not mean they are cultic in the abusive sense. However, like any religion they can become cultic depending on how each is administered to individuals.

For cultism, abuses are the keys. For orthodoxy the basic tenets of the Christian faith are the keys. You analyse. You decide.

Alamo Christian Church

The Alamo Christian Church in Saugus, California, began, according to its leaders Tony and Susan Alamo, on the streets of Hollywood. While the church expanded to Dyer, Arkansas, several trusted followers were left to run the group in Saugus, Tony and Susan having left California. The church observes a strict legalism and separation from other Christian groups. Ex-members also report that a highly structured hierarchy exists. Approval is gained through prayer, and a rigid work system. It has produced television programmes to promote its activities and also published many tracts to gain new converts. In 1974 the California State Senate Select Committee on Children and Youth looked into several religious movements, this one included, and heard testimony on mind control, inadequate living conditions, and other manipulative activities from ex-members. Susan died several years ago of cancer. According to Professor Ronald Enroth, Alamo has received notoriety recently for its 'outrageous anti-Catholic tracts'.

Baha'i

In 1844 this splinter Islamic group arose to replace Muhammad's revelation from God with a new one. Today it exists as the Baha'i faith, named after Baha'u'llah, an early leader in the splinter group. The Baha'i mission is to bring all religions, peoples, governments, and nations together through its particular faith. Building on Muhammad's claim that each age needed its own prophet, the Baha'i leaders felt they represented the new interpreters of God for the nineteenth and twentieth centuries. Much of the doctrine is similar to Islam and individual responsibility is worked out through duties close to the concepts contained in the Five Pillars of Islam. Based in Haifa, Israel, a nine-person board currently oversees the Baha'i faith throughout the world.

Bhagwan Shree Rajneesh

While the USA can claim it is no longer troubled by the physical presence of Bhagwan Shree (the god) Rajneesh, his tumultuous departure from the States leaves many questions about him open to the rest of the world where 500,000 devotees still follow him: questions because of his bizarre beliefs, tirades against all other religions and religious leaders, his living in opulence, his frank desire for money and his advocacy of free and open sex.

The Oregon commune, 64,000-acre Big Muddy Ranch, is dissolving now that the Bhagwan has left the USA under a deportation agreement with US and Oregon State law and justice officials who had brought various felony charges against him. In agreeing to leave the US and to pay a $400,000 fine, Rajneesh pleaded guilty to two federal immigration charges. Most of his devotees seemed unaffected by his pleading guilty to crimes and his flight from America. His impact on the world religious scene appears to be dwindling at least while he wanders the globe trying once again to find a more permanent place to come to rest. Many nations such as Greece and Ireland have rebuffed his attempts to settle. Presently the Bhagwan lives in Bombay, India. If he finds citizenship or permanent residency in a non-hostile nation his prominence may once again be felt. His 'orange people' still follow him despite his physical absence.

Born 11 December, 1931 in India, Rajneesh received an MA in Philosophy from Saugur University in 1957. Between 1964 and 1969 he struggled to instruct his students in the elementary techniques of enlightenment. By 1981 some 8,000 people had come to sit at the feet of this exciting new guru at his international headquarters in Poona, India. Jetsetters, the wealthy and cultural elite from Europe and the US, quickly made the 'holy man' popular throughout the world. In 1981 he moved to the United States and embarked on his plan to establish an 'enlightened community' in Antelope, Oregon.

Basically, Rajneesh teaches hedonism or self-indulgent pursuit of pleasure. He couches this modern epicurianism ('eat, drink and be merry for tomorrow we die') in his own form of Hinduism with teachings and techniques from Zen Buddhism and various forms of pop psychology. He is a monist:

God, creation and man are all one with no ultimate distinctions between them. Rajneesh describes God as a process, not a personal being. However, Rajneesh clearly becomes the voice of God and a god to his followers. He himself took on the title 'Bhagwan Shree', meaning God.

The cult's hedonism had been extreme to the point of reports of open orgies, rapes, beatings and abandonment of children. Some of his followers such as his former lieutenant, the combative 'Ma' Sheela Silverman, are facing criminal charges including attempted murder. Followers see Rajneesh's legal troubles as only persecution from 'bigots' in Oregon and the US government. The Bhagwan attributes none of the charges and hedonistic abusiveness to himself but now blames Sheela and other disenchanted former Rajneeshpuram (Antelope commune) leaders.

Under his philosophy life is to be playful and one's goal is to be 'blissed-out' without regard to others' misfortunes. Such 'bliss' is only obtained by denying the real world where sin, sorrow and suffering are obvious.

Enlightenment is obtained through sex, marriage is a bondage and a chain while families are a 'rotten' social group and must be forsaken. Two primary requirements for the status of true discipleship are the surrender to Rajneesh's teaching and complete acceptance of his words.

Buddhism

Also springing from India, Buddhism seeks to free man from wrong thinking and wrong living through the Noble Eight-fold Path: right views, right aspirations, right speech, right conduct, right mode of livelihood, right effort, right mindfulness, and right rapture, 'as originated from the teachings of Siddartha Gautama Buddha. The word Buddha is a title meaning 'enlightened one'.

Born a prince in 503 BC, Siddartha became dismayed at seeing the harshness of life that existed beyond the walls of his father's palace. He left the palace and became a holy man practising traditional Hinduism. He became dissatisfied with the idea of the reincarnation cycle and he searched for a means to gain freedom from it without having to keep returning. He eventually succeeded and achieved enlightenment.

Buddhism denies the existence of any God; it has no theology. Karma still determines the number of reincarnations and karma is believed to be an impersonal force. His teachings assert it is our own activity that determines our incarnation. Therefore man is responsible for both his condemnation to reincarnation and his deliverance from the cycle. Its main appeal lies in its sense of personal responsibility as the means of reaching enlightenment.

Christian Science

Using the teachings of Mary Baker Eddy, the founder of Christian Science, her followers deny the reality of evil, refuse to acknowledge the existence of misery, and claim death is an illusion, the fears produced by a mind wrapped in ignorance.

Born in 1821, Baker claimed in 1866 to have fallen on ice, been declared hopelessly crippled, and then healed by her own powers on the third day of her suffering. While the attending physician denied under oath to have ever diagnosed her conditions as irreversible, Baker went on to claim that she had received a special revelation into the human condition and did her best to promote her findings.

In her works she denied the personhood of God; God is Principle, Love, Spirit, Intelligence, but not a being. She also refuted the inspiration of the Bible, the Trinity, the virgin birth of Jesus, miracles, the atonement of Jesus Christ, his ascension and second coming, Satan, evil, hell, the kingdom of heaven, eternal salvation, the biblical understanding of prayer, man's origin from dust, sin, sickness and death.

Church of Bible Understanding

Denial of the Trinity marks some of the familiar differences between the Church of Bible Understanding and orthodox Christianity. The founder, Stewart Traill, claims his interpretation of scriptures is the only interpretation. Members are asked to leave families in order to live with other members, surrender all funds, and report to Traill on other members' activities. Traill also may be transferring his USA-based movement to Haiti where a small group of Foundation members are located. While he enjoyed a 3,000 membership list in the nineteen-seventies, gained through an aggressive street evangelism, by 1980 the church had dwindled to 700 followers.

Church Universal and Triumphant

In 1958 Mark L. Prophet began the Church Universal And Triumphant, also known as the Summit Lighthouse. Prophet based his organisation on occultic practices of spiritism, the conversing with spirit beings, and claims to have contacted Confucius, Buddha, Jesus, Jesus' mother, and Saint Francis, all of whom approve of his activities. Church Universal denies the specific identity of Jesus, that he is exclusively the Son of God. Prophet emphasised that the works of Jesus were models for everyone to follow, difficult exercises that would eventually lead to spiritual enlightenment and individual godhead. Although Prophet died in 1973 his wife continues to oversee the church through conferences, various publications, and classes at the Summit University in Malibu, California.

Divine Light Mission

Divine Light Mission (DLM) recruits mainly through personal contacts where invitations are made to attend meetings. At the initial gathering many songs are sung, more literature is available, and further information is promised later at another meeting. Guru Maharaj Ji is the main figure of DLM. He requires total submission to teachings. Often the hopeful trainee must follow the guru from place to place before finally being granted an audience with the spiritual leader. As in Hinduism, DLM discounts the cognitive abilities of the mind for understanding experience; the mind cannot get past the great illusion of separation. DLM promotes four activities to gain enlightenment: meditation, observing the guru, spiritual teaching, and service. The guru also requires devotees to donate gifts and possessions in order to become real followers. DLM operates through ashrams, places that house and employ followers.

Eckankar

Eckankar, the Ancient Science of Soul Travel, began in 1964. The now worldwide movement is based in Las Vegas, Nevada.

Paul Twitchell founded Eckankar through a series of lectures and articles based on his philosophy of out-of-the-body travel. Later he claimed to be the incarnation of God and that Eckankar actually began earlier than 1964, somewhere in the dawn of humanity. Salvation (or more simply, the end goal in Eckankar) can be achieved only with the aid of a living Eck Master. The movement borrows heavily from Hinduism in that God is all, life is ruled by karma, and the presence of a guru is needed. Eckankar promotes itself through tapes, literature and membership dues. It recruits primarily through newspaper advertisements.

Hinduism

Hinduism claims primordial origins and has no specific founder. While to the western civilisations it is most noted as the religion of India, Hinduism offers more than spiritual solutions to man's questions about himself and his existence. Moral, social, cultural, and ethical concepts and practices are woven into Hinduism so that a believer's life is fully regimented about what to eat and wear, where to work, and whom to marry.

This regimentation is worked out through five basic social divisions: Brahmans (priests), Kshatriyas (warriors), Vaisayas (merchants and farmers), Sudras (workers), and Panchamas (the 'untouchables'). A person is born into his or her caste, and while there may be great upward mobility in particular castes there is no graduation from one caste to another in this life. Reincarnation then serves an important role in moving from caste to caste toward the final incarnation before escaping from the cyle of birth-death-and-rebirth.

After death a person's works or deeds (karma) in life determine the next step in the cycle. Salvation or enlightenment in Hinduism comes to the male, the Indian male to be exact. Females, foreign males, and animals must be reborn as Hindu males in order to achieve release from the lengthy cycle.

Hindus believe that God is one, but that deity manifests itself in many forms and that those forms are given great honour as distinct revelations of God's oneness. To the Hindu there is nothing that is not God; no real separation exists between

Creator and creation. Any doctrine of separation is considered illusion. This theology is called monism. The ultimate reality of Hinduism is to see through the illusion and return to the oneness in that individual that is also God.

Hindus divide their writings into two groups: Shruti, which is God originated, and Smirti, which is also God originated but handed down through men.

Islam

In Islam all activities take root from the concept of total submission. The word itself actually means 'submission'.

'There is no God but God, and Muhammad is his prophet.' Through Islam Muhammad, an Arab merchant who lived around 610 AD, claimed that according to the angel Gabriel he was the last prophet from a line that included Noah, Abraham, Moses and Jesus. While Muhammad's mission was to return the Arabs to the worship of the one true God (of their father Abraham, through his son Ishmael, not Isaac) he also denied the deity of Jesus, and the Trinity — tenets which brought (and still bring) opposition from orthodox Christianity.

As the message was revealed to him Muhammad learned that each age was to have its own special prophet, Muhammad being the last. He appeared well suited for the mission. He sought economic and social reforms through the words God had given him to speak. These efforts were the reason that many of his sermons were originally rejected by his own countrymen.

In its single major work the *Qu'ran*, Islam teaches that all people are personally responsible for their actions and are delivered by God through the observance of the Five Pillars: confession of faith, daily prayers, fasting, giving alms, and making a pilgrimage to Mecca, the holy city of Islamic faith. Salvation comes about by the working out of the duties involved in the Five Pillars and submission to them is considered a sign of great personal piety. Worship is done individually. Each person is considered to be alone before God during that time. Although many may be seen praying together, their prayers and acts of devotion are personal and separate.

Jehovah's Witnesses

Fifty years after Joseph Smith had translated 'the golden tablets' that were to become the inspiration of the Mormon Church, Charles Taze Russel founded 'Zion's Watch Tower'. In eighty-four years this magazine went from 6,000 to 64,000,000 in circulation and is the main voice of the Jehovah's Witnesses, the name given to the group under its second leader, Joseph Rutherford.

Russel claimed to have found the true meaning of the Bible, meaning that orthodox Christianity was hopelessly in error. Denying the Trinity, the personality of the Holy Spirit, the deity of Jesus, his bodily resurrection, his visible return, and the reality of hell, Russel's movement grew despite constant court battles waged to disprove his authority for making such claims. (The Witnesses suffered a serious setback in 1975 when the prediction of the world's end in that year did not occur.)

Since their inception Jehovah's Witnesses have published materials in 92 countries and over 110 translations of its literature are promoted to different lands. They have missionary programmes in 214 countries. In their witnessing the missionaries rarely identify themselves as Jehovah's Witnesses until they are assured of the person's possible conversion.

Latter-day Saints (Mormons)

Latter-day Saints began in the first half of the nineteenth century in the USA under the leadership of Joseph Smith. At present over 4,500,000 members in 83 different countries study *The Book of Mormon* which was first copyrighted on 11 June, 1829. Missionaries continue witnessing daily through door-to-door evangelism to increase their number.

According to the group's history, Smith was visited in 1820 by God the Father and God the Son and told not to join any other established church. In 1823 the angel Moroni (the son of Mormon) appeared to Smith and told him where to find the golden plates from which *The Book of Mormon* originated. It is the doctrinal statements springing from this work that traditionally have separated Mormons from orthodox Christianity.

God as exalted man, our human potential for becoming God, and the Aaronic/Melchizedekian priesthoods are a few of the doctrines the Saints hold (but are nowhere to be found in the original 1829 manuscripts or in Christendom).

Despite these and other differences, the Saints, who refer to themselves as Christians, promote selfless dedication and work to increase stability in the family structure, attractive ideas to potential members. Although missionaries use the Bible in their witnessing, it is a text specially annotated to explain Mormon beliefs. Persons familiar with the scriptures find it difficult to confront what appear to be slightly different interpretations, and they often succumb to the friendly presentation and positive programmes.

The church itself is governed by the First Presidency, then the Council of Twelve, followed by the First Council of Seventy, and Bishops who are in charge of local church 'wards'. The main headquarters are in Salt Lake City, Utah, USA.

Scientology

In the nineteen-forties writer L. Ron Hubbard began to practice 'dianetics', a programme designed to provide therapy for mind improvement. By making patients aware of unwanted behaviour patterns, dianetics promised to help them get rid of any neuroses. By 1952 the movement had moved into occultish beliefs and spiritual areas by accepting the possibility of reincarnation. Dianetics then became Scientology. Through written materials, seminars, and original dianetic therapy Scientologists claimed to gain a self-knowledge that included past-life existence, soul travel, mastery over the Material-Energy-Space-Time universe, and the ability to escape to the next plane of reality.

The Forum

Werner Erhard and Associates, formerly Erhard Seminars Training or EST, now also known as 'The Forum', seeks to change an individual's understanding of self and environment by exchanging that knowledge for a lifestyle grounded in self and an environment grounded in a belief in an impersonal divinity.

EST or est was founded by Erhard in the nineteen-seventies

after experimenting in areas of Scientology, Mind Dynamics, Zen Buddhism, hypnosis, Subud, Yoga, psycho-cybernetics, Gestalt, encounter therapy, and transpersonal psychology.

EST recruits individuals mainly through personal invitations to attend weekend seminars. Average attendance numbers around 250 people who are 'voluntarily' subjected to 16 to 20 continuous hours of lecture with few, if any, breaks. Previous beliefs and convictions are broken down by the trainer through alternating humour, accusation, meditation, abusive language, intimidation, and interrogation. Audience participation is limited to exchanges between trainer and individual; no verbal communication is allowed among members of the audience. Every effort is made to keep the individual's attention on the trainer's presentation and not his or her own thoughts.

In 1979 EST had 160,000 graduates. By 1981 325,000 people had been 'trained' around the world with the number now between 500,000 and a million. As Erhard's final goal is the elimination of any prior beliefs, EST is hostile to all other beliefs or philosophies. Trainers claim EST will enhance your present beliefs while adherents have said you can have EST and Jesus Christ at the same time. EST teaches reality is only experienced and created through personal experience. Being strongly humanistic, God is no longer the centre of one's life and the universe but rather man or the individual is the master of his existence.

During the transformation of EST into 'the Forum', Erhard's teachings have drifted into an emphasis on personal success and monetary gain.

Transcendental Meditation

In 1954 Maharishi Mahesh Yogi founded Transcendental Meditation (TM). To be precise, TM found him in a cave where the idea to simplify the practice of attaining a higher level of consciousness came to him after his living in seclusion for two years.

Although TM has been promoted as a scientifically credible, non-religious method for self-improvement, as its popularity increased so did the awareness that the easy techniques TM advocated were tied directly to Hindu monism.

Initial meetings begin innocently enough. Advertisements in the form of posters or flyers placed in libraries, schools, and other public places promise a free meeting where an introductory presentation of TM's benefits are offered. The TM instructor lays out the claims. TM offers easy, scientifically proven ways to achieve mental relaxation and develop full individual potential.

At the second meeting the participants pay instruction fees ($250 adults, $150 student, and advanced TM/SIDHI $3,000). After this TM slides into its religious roots with a Hindu prayer to a particular manifestation of the divine being. TM participants are carefully lured into accepting Maharishi's monist beliefs despite the fact that TM continues to claim it is a non-religious organisation.

Unification Church

Born on 6 January, 1920, Sun Myung Moon, founder of 'The Holy Spirit Association for the Unification of World Christianity', grew up in Korea at a time when belief in a Korean messiah was popular in the underground Pentecostal Church. In 1946 Moon began the 'Broad Sea Church' in Pyongyang. Eight years later he started the 'Unification Church' in Seoul by declaring himself to be the new messenger of God who would save the world and unify it under his leadership. Publication of his *Divine Principle* followed. A revised English translation was printed in the United States in 1966 and 1973. In 1972 Moon claimed to receive a message from God that he should bring his ministry to the United States. He currently resides in New York State. He has completed a US Federal prison sentence for income tax evasion.

Divine Principle contains the core of Moon's doctrine. As God's new messenger his goal is to bring the world together under himself. Moon claims the new revelation supersedes traditional New Testament theology. In order to achieve this Moon asserts that Jesus was to unify mankind, only the crucifixion interrupted his plans. Moon believes Jesus only achieved a partial redemption; Moon himself teaches he is the messiah to completely save mankind.

Salvation comes to followers through their recruitment efforts. Invitations to dinner follow personal encounters. Throughout the gathering no opportunities are allowed for guests to be alone; a believer is always present to bring any thoughts back to focus on the goals of the Unification Church. The next step is attending a retreat workshop. Again little individual response among initiates is allowed. Schedules are tight for all activities, from eating to lecturing. No time is provided for reflection. The urge to conform is constantly enforced.

Final indoctrination has included giving away all possessions (to the church), an act that makes the new member completely dependent upon older members. Anyone not in the church is automatically under Satan's control, especially family and friends. Diet changes have in the past reportedly been demanded. Acceptance is earned through recruitment of outsiders. All these activities are required for individual salvation which increases the level of personal involvement with Moon's whole programme. According to some sources the church has been going through a transition and reports of abuses have dwindled.

Membership of the church is somewhere between 300,000 and 500,000 people. Japan and Korea contain the highest number of members.

Way International

The Way International, founded by the late Victor Paul Wierwille in the USA, uses a personal approach to witnessing. Wierwille assembled the 'Power for Abundant Living' course where potential converts are put through a cycle of exercise, work and fellowship that allows little time for individual inquiry. The Way Corps, headquarters assignments, and 'the Word over the World' (WOW) programme serve as an introductory means to membership. The cost of the 'Power' course has often been as high as $100. Persons unable to pay are considered unfit for teaching and future membership. Followers of The Way reject the Trinity, Jesus' deity, and other traditions Wierwille claims have crept in since the writings of the apostle Paul. True worship is also recognised by the practice of spiritual gifts.

Worldwide Church of God

Herbert W. Armstrong, recently deceased founder of the Worldwide Church of God, began his church after leaving a splinter group, the Church of God, over his acceptance of Anglo-Israelism, a belief which claims the nations of England and the USA are the true descendants of the ten lost tribes of Israel.

The Worldwide Church, formerly called the Radio Church of God, is marked by many observances borrowed from other religious movements: seventh day sabbath, abstinence from certain 'unclean' foods (Seventh Day Adventists); denial of the Trinity and Jesus' bodily resurrection (Jehovah's Witnesses); and that man may become God (Mormonism), besides having their own extreme legalism, denial of hell and eternal punishment, and the already mentioned Anglo-Israelism. Armstrong promoted these teachings through the Church's main publication, *The Plain Truth* (circulation 1,292,000), his 'the World Tomorrow Programme' on radio, and two colleges, the Ambassador College in Pasadena, California, and in St Albans, Hertfordshire, England. It is mostly through these efforts that new members are contacted and indoctrinated.

Epilogue

We are seekers. We are social beings.

Commitment to a cause should only be made when two conditions have been met: first, there should be a knowledge of the facts; second, the cause should be based on truth — the religious and philosophic concepts should be true and the organisation should be honest.

Christians need never compromise themselves intellectually, spiritually or morally. Jesus claimed that his teaching is truth. The test of Christianity's truthfulness should be the same as we use for belonging to any group or forming any relationship. Christians should be prepared to be scrutinised, questioned and evaluated as to whether or not they are living out the truth they claim is in them. This is the point of the following words from Isaiah 52:5 quoted by Paul to the Christians at Rome: 'For the name of God is blasphemed among the Gentiles because of you [those people who were not living out what they were preaching to others] just as it is written' (Romans 2:24).

If a group is based on truth, it should not have to implement cultic deceptions and abuses to get or keep members. The truth can appeal and draw commitments on its own merits. Failing to realise this, many organisations fall prey to using dishonest tactics to gain and hold converts.

We should keep our minds open so that we are enabled to ask well-thought-out questions and not settle for superficial answers. The quality of fruit is not always obvious; and in harvesting it we are the ones who must taste its sweetness or bitterness. We should plant orchards until we eat the harvest that satisfies our hunger. For that work we are responsible.

Appendix A

Annotated bibliography of literature related to new religious movements

This bibliography has been prepared by Spiritual Counterfeits Project staff in response to the significant number of inquiries we have received concerning various subjects, groups and individuals. We trust that it will aid you in securing information about and discerning the essential thrust of particular teachings from a biblical perspective. At the same time, we feel it wise to advise you that some treatments are no more than cursory examinations, intended only to answer basic questions. To extract the greatest value from this bibliography, use it as a base for both your own research and your own sensitive dialogue with adherents of particular groups or movements.

An additional word is in order. Almost without exception, New Age, occult and Eastern spiritual groups have at their core a secret, experience-based teaching which is accessible only to initiates of the group. This esoteric level of knowledge is rarely represented in the materials which the group makes available to the public. In fact, in many cases the private teaching actually contradicts the public representation of the group's beliefs. The research of some of these authors may be based on a study of such a group's outer precepts, rather than on an understanding of their esoteric doctrines.

It should also be noted that the Spiritual Counterfeits Project does not necessarily endorse or agree with every viewpoint expressed in the books which are listed. Listed publications have been chosen primarily as sources of helpful information and secondarily as helpful evaluations. It is hoped that the brief annotations of each book will help the reader determine a given author's spiritual stance and make allowances for it.

Bibliography with subject titles and annotations

1. Adam, Ben, *Astrology: The Ancient Conspiracy*, abridged ed., Dimension Books/ Bethany Fellowship Press, 1963, pb, 112 pp.

Astrology

Four essays, originally an English publication titled *The Origins of Heathendom*. Only one essay deals directly with astrology, relating it to knowledge of divine grace given by the Lord to Adam and then corrupted as humankind was scattered over the earth. Second edition (1964) uses original title.

2. Anderson, Roy A., *Secrets of the Spirit World*, Pacific Press Publishing Association, 1966, pb, 92 pp.

Spiritism

A popular admonitory account in the light of Christian teaching of the writer's encounters with spiritistic phenomena through friends and others.

3. Bjornstad, James, *The Moon is Not the Son*, Dimension Books/Bethany Fellowship Press, 1976, pb, 126 pp., appendices, bibliography, notes.

Moon, Rev. Sun Myung

Taoist philosophy, Christian words and phrases, Bible verses, spiritism, numerology, physics and anticommunism are all part of the eclectic emphases of the Unification Church founded by Rev. Sun Myung Moon. Contents include chapters on Moon's history, claims and theology (contrasting it with biblical doctrines). Brief quotation from *Master Speaks*, and an ex-Moonie's testimony reprinted from *Alternatives* magazine. One of the better books on Moon.

4. Bjornstad, James, *The Transcendental Mirage*, Dimension Books/Bethany Fellowship Press, 1976, pb, 93 pp., appendices, bibliography, notes.

Transcendental Meditation

Brief treatment of TM by an early observer who documents its changing self-presentation from religious to secular and points out its differences from the gospel. A Christian approach.

5. Bjornstad, James, *Twentieth Century Prophecy*, Dimension Books/Bethany Fellowship Press, 1969, pb, 140 pp., appendices, book reviews, notes.

a. Cayce, Edgar

b. Dixon, Jeane

Discussion (65 pp.) of why Dixon cannot be considered a valid prophet of God, her psychic powers notwithstanding, in light of biblical definitions of the prophetic role. Comparison of Cayce's clairvoyant 'readings' with the teachings of scripture (70 pp.) showing them to be mutually exclusive.

6. Blankenship, Roberta, *Escape from Witchcraft*, Zondervan Publishing House, 1972, pb, 114 pp.

Witchcraft

Personal story of a young girl who got into witchcraft, then was led to Christ by a Youth for

Christ worker. First section is, regrettably, somewhat more gripping.

7. Box, Bart J. and Lawrence E. Jerome, *Objections to Astrology*, Impact Series/Prometheus Books, 1975, pb, 62 pp.
Astrology
Short statement on astrology's lack of a scientific basis, signed by 192 scientists (including 19 Nobel Prize winners), plus two readable essays by the authors. All three parts originally appeared in *The Humanist*.

8. Author unknown, *B.O.O.K. (Beliefs of Other Kinds)*, Kate Ellen Gruver, ed., Southern Baptist Convention, n.d., magazine format, 128 pp.
a. Armstrong, Herbert W.
b Baha'i
c Jehovah's Witnesses
d Muslims
e Nichiren Buddhism
f Occultism
g Satanism
h Spiritism
i The Unitarian Church
j Unity School of Christianity
k Witchcraft
l Zen Buddhism
An understanding guide to aggressive but not offensive witness to friends who espouse nonevangelical faith systems. One article on each topic, along with a Baptist view of Judaism and Roman Catholicism/Eastern Orthodoxy. 8-1/2 x 11, good photos.

9. Braemer, Alice, *Cultism to Charisma*, Exposition Press, 1977, hb, 44 pp.
Dixon, Jeane
Brief, somewhat scattered testimony of a woman influenced by Unity and Christian Science who worked for Jeane Dixon for seven years, then became a Christian through the '700 Club'. The author is now active in charismatic circles.

10. Breese, Dave, *Know the Marks of Cults*, Victor Books, 1975, pb, 128 pp.
Examines twelve basic errors of false religion.
Short chapters on the typical errors of the nearly endless list of cults existing in our time. The author, associated with 'Back to the Bible Broadcast', discusses such general characteristics as extrabiblical revelation, false basis of salvation, presumptuous messianic leadership, defective Christology, enslaving organisational structure, denunciation of others, etc.

11. Brooke, Tal, *Lord of the Air*, abridged ed., Lion Publishing, 1976, hb, 189 pp.
Sai Baba or Sri Sathya Sai Baba
Personal account of a young man's search for truth first through drugs, then through Eastern mysticism and finally through Christ. Brooke describes his 17-month commitment in India to a 'master' named Sai Baba and his shocked disillusionment when Baba's sexual proclivities toward his male disciples came to light. Encouragingly, Brooke's life was touched by Christian missionaries at just that time. (Note: an unabridged

edition of *Lord of the Air* is available from Vikas Publishing House Pvt Ltd, 1979, hb, 424 pp., appendix, index.)

12. Burrell, Maurice C. and H. Stafford Wright, *Whom Then Can We Believe?*, Moody Press, 1976, pb, 128 pp.

a Armstrong, Herbert W.
b Christadelphianism
c Christian Science
d Jehovah's Witnesses
e The Mormon Church
f Satanism
g Spiritualism
h Witchcraft

Brief discussions of various modern belief systems vaguely related to Christianity but before the cult explosion of the 1960+ period. Five pages on 'religions of inner experience'; four pages on the 'Christian belief in the Trinity', the latter often the crux of a group's aberration. This book was originally published as *Some Modern Faiths* (1973) by InterVarsity in England.

13. Campbell, Roger F., *Herbert W. Armstrong and His Worldwide Church of God*, Christian Literature Crusade, 1974, pb, 129 pp., index, notes.

Armstrong, Herbert W.

Nine chapters dealing with specific areas where Armstrong departs from orthodox Bible-teaching. A well-documented attempt to help those who 'want out' of Armstrongism.

14. Chang, Lit-sen, *Zen-Existentialism: The Spiritual Decline of the West*, Presbyterian and Reformed Publishing Co., 1969, hb, 201 pp., appendices, glossary, index.

a Drugs
b Existentialism
c Zen

Lengthy study in lecture form of today's spiritual climate; the history, nature, teachings and practice of Zen; and the impact of Zen on the West, culturally, philosophically, religiously and theologically. The author, once a follower of Zen, has been a special lecturer in missions at Gordon Divinity School. Both the book and an epilogue are subtitled *A Positive Answer to the Hippies*. Appendices by Hudston T. Armerding, Wheaton College President, and Carl F.H. Henry.

15. Author unknown, *Christ or the Lodge?*, Kuiper, R.B. et al., Great Commission Publications, 1942, pb, 23 pp.

Freemasonry

Booklet based on a 1942 report to the General Assembly of the Orthodox Presbyterian Church. Concludes that membership in the Masonic fraternity is inconsistent with Christianity.

16. Author unknown, *Christian Witness Among Muslims*, Africa Christian Press, 1971, pb, 96 pp., appendix, bibliography.

Muslims, especially in Africa

Short handbook for African Christians who are in a position to witness to Muslims. A brief introduction to Islam with discussion questions. Well-outlined with good summaries and sensitive practical advice.

17. Clark, David K., *The Pantheism of Alan Watts*, InterVarsity Press, 1978, pb, 118 pp., bibliography, notes Watts, Alan

A study of Watts, once an Anglican priest, who abandoned Christianity for Eastern thought (having found Christianity 'uncompromising, ornery, militant, rigorous, imperious and invincibly self-righteous'). A readable well-annotated critique of the conceptual difficulties of pantheism and Eastern philosophies (especially Zen) as the basis for a world view.

18. Clements, R.D., *God and the Gurus*, InterVarsity Press, 1975, pb, 64 pp., appendix, notes.

a Divine Light Mission
b Hare Krishna movement
c Mysticism
d Transcendental Meditation

Booklet on the basic elements of Eastern thought and its challenges, plus short chapters on specific groups. An appendix on practical advice to Christians when dealing with Eastern mystical groups.

19. Downing, Jim, *Meditation: The Bible Tells You How*, NavPress, 1976, pb, 96 pp.

An explanation of authentic Christian meditation

An exhortation and guide to Bible study, meditation on the Word and the devotional life. It also discusses the place of the mind, affections and will in the fruitful Christian life. The author is active with the Navigators.

20. Enroth, Ronald, *Youth, Brainwashing and the Extremist Cults*, Zondervan Publishing House, 1977, pb, 221 pp., index.

a Alamo Christian Foundation
b Children of God
c Cultic commitment
d Divine Light Mission
e Hare Krishna movement
f The Love Family
g The plight of parents
h Satan's part in false religion
i Seduction of youth by cults
j The Unification Church
k The Way

Case studies (150 pp.) based on extensive interviews with ex-cultists, who in some cases were abducted from the cult by their parents and then deprogrammed. Insightful commentary (70 pp.) by the author, a Westmont College (Calif.) sociologist. Some information on groups for parents whose children are in cults.

21. Evans, Dr Christopher, *Cults of Unreason*, Farrar, Straus and Giroux, 1973, pb, 158 pp., index

a. Aetherius Society
b. Atlantis
c. E-meters
d. Gurdjieff
e. Hare Krishna movement
f. Krishnamurti
g. The Process Church
h. Scientology
i. Subud
j. Theosophy
k. UFOs
l. Yoga

Study of the proliferation of surrogate belief-systems that rise to power when (according to the author), as a result of the onslaught of science, 'the great world religions offer only outdated, timeworn and implausible concepts'. Most space is given to Scientology, regarded as the most important and disturbing belief-system. Forty pages are devoted to UFOs which are portrayed as an important sociological phenomenon and another 30 pages deal with 'black-box' groups who are preoccupied with quasi-scientific gadgetry.

22. Gasson, Raphael, *The Changing Counterfeit*, Pyramid Publications for Logos International, 1970, pb, 160 pp.

a. Clairaudience
b. Clairvoyance
d. Psychometry
d. Spiritualism (Spiritism)

Autobiography plus history and popular critique of spiritualism by a former medium, now a Christian. One chapter on the 'Christian Spiritualist' movement; other chapters on spiritualist phenomena and their dangers (healing, 'rescue work', 'physical' mediumship, materialisation). Gasson disappeared some years ago and has never publicly verified the claims presented in this book.

23. Goodspeed, Edgar J., *Famous 'Biblical' Hoaxes*, Twin Brooks Series, Baker Book House, 1956, pb, 124 pp., index.

a. The Aquarian Gospel of Jesus the Christ
b. The Book of Jasher
c. The Confession of Pontius Pilate
d. The Crucifixion of Jesus, by an Eyewitness
e. The Death Warrant of Jesus Christ
f. The Description of Christ
g. The Gospel of Josephus
h. The Letter of Benan
i. The Letter from Heaven
j. The Long-Lost Second Book of Acts
k. The Lost Books of the Bible
l. The Nazarene Gospel
m. Oahspe
n. The Report of Pilate
o. The Twenty-ninth Chapter of Acts
p. The Unknown Life of Jesus Christ

An in-depth expose, by an early 20th-century Bible scholar/translator, of various misleading writings that claim to be translations of early Christian documents. The author points out that these documents do not meet the tests of antiquity and genuineness, but rather are curious frauds 'dredged up from obscure depths mostly beyond the ken of educated people'. First published (1931) under the title *Modern Apocrypha*. Excellent.

24. Gruss, Edmond C., *Cults and the Occult in the Age of Aquarius*, Baker Book House, 1974, pb, 132 pp.

a. Armstrong, Herbert W.
b. Astrology
c. Baha'i
d. Cayce, Edgar and the A.R.E.
e. Christian Science
f. Jehovah's Witnesses

g. The Mormon Church
h. Occultism
i. Ouija boards
j. Rosicrucianism
k. Scientology
l. Spiritualism (Spiritism)
m. Unity School of Christianity

Brief popular introduction to the cult phenomenon in general; short chapters on specific groups in particular, along with succinct conclusions and a bibliography on each.

25. Gruss, Edmond C., *What About the Ouija Board?*, Moody Press, 1973, pb, 16 pp., notes.
Ouija boards
Small booklet discussing the history and current popularity of the ouija board. Discusses the natural, possibly supernatural, forces that 'make it work' and the dangers of occult entrapment.

26. Guinness, Os, 'The East, No Exit', chapter 6 in *The Dust of Death*, InterVarsity Press, 1973, pb, 419 pp., references; *Encircling Eyes*, InterVarsity Press, 1974, pb, 54 pp., notes, recommended further reading. (Note: also chapter 8 in *The Dust of Death*.)
a. Eastern mysticism
b. Occultism
Why a generation disillusioned with the West has searched for an alternative in the East; and why many of them have returned disappointed and disillusioned. Discussion of the resurgent trend toward perverse religiosity and the occult (superstition, spiritism, Satanism), along with the Christian position. Well- annotated for original sources.

27. Haddon, David, *Transcendental Meditation: A Christian View*, InterVarsity Press, 1975, pb, 30 pp., notes, recommended further reading.
Transcendental Meditation
Short introductory booklet directed to students. 'We should seriously consider the possibility that the suspension of conscious direction of the faculties in meditation opens one to Satanic spiritual influences.' Evangelistic conclusion.

28. Haddon, David and Vail Hamilton, *T.M. Wants You!*, Baker Book House, 1976, pb, 204 pp., notes.
Transcendental Meditation
An interesting, careful study of the theology, philosophy and claims of TM by a former Spiritual Counterfeits Project researcher and a former TM instructor. Chapters in a question-and-answer format on the movement, practice, scientific view, faith and enlightenment, Maharishi's theology in Christian perspective and a Christian response. This book is the most substantial treatment of TM from a Christian perspective.

29. Haldeman, I.M. *Can the Dead Communicate with the Living?*, Direction Books/Baker Book House, 1976, pb, 138 pp.
Spiritism
Short treatment that attempts to be objective and thorough on

what the Bible says about spiritism. Written after World War I, now reprinted. Reflects the style of an earlier era (at times sentimental and preachy), but still helpful.

30. Hanna, Mark, *The True Path: Seven Muslims Make Their Greatest Discovery*, International Doorways Publishers, 1975, pb, 154 pp., appendices, bibliography, glossary.

Testimonies of Muslims who have become Christians

Personal accounts of individuals who became Christians out of Muslim backgrounds, then were viewed as religious apostates, moral lepers and (in some countries) political traitors. An epilogue, glossary and appendices are directed to inquiring Muslims.

31. Hefley, James C., *The Youthnappers*, Victor Books, 1977, pb, 208 pp., appendix.

a. Armageddon, Church of
b Baba, Meher
c Baha'i
d Bhajan, Yogi
e The Body
f Brother Evangelist
g Brother Julius's followers
h Children of God (The Family of Love)
i Divine Light Mission
j Eckankar
k Esalen
l est
m Free John, Bubba
n Hare Krishna movement
o Holy Order of MANS
p Inner-Light Foundation
q Integral Yoga Institute (Swami Satchidananda)
r Intercosmic Center of Spiritual Associations
s LeGrand, Bishop Devernon
t The Local Church
u Moon, Rev Sun Myung
v Preventative for the cults
w Satan worship (Anton LaVey)
x Scientology
y Self-Realisation Fellowship
z Soka-gakkai (Value Creation Society)
aa Subud
bb Transcendental Meditation
cc The Way
dd World Messianity-Johrei, Church of
ee Zen

Popular analysis of controversial groups, their origins, beliefs, leadership, methods and goals. Brief discussion of parental concerns, deprogramming and why American youths are receptive to beliefs and practices inimical to their upbringing.

32. Hesselgrave, David J., ed., *Dynamic Religious Movements*, Baker Book House, 1978, hb, 326 pp., notes

a Jehovah's Witnesses
b Jesus Only movement
c Moon, Rev Sun Myung
d The Mormon Church
e Nichiren Buddhism

Chapters, by various writers, described as case studies of growing religious movements around the world. Only Jehovah's Witnesses and Mormonism are treated in North America. Lengthy sociological conclusion, 'What Causes Religious Movements to Grow' by the author.

33. Hinson, William B., *The Broadway (sic) to Armageddon*, Religion in the News, 1977, pb, 234 pp.

Armstrong, Herbert W.

Colloquial autobiographical account by a minister who spent 14 years in the Worldwide Church of God. Much miscellaneous emotional detail; poorly edited and proofread.

34. Hoekema, Anthony A., *The Four Major Cults*, Wm. B. Eerdmans Publishing Co., 1963, hb, 447 pp., bibliography, index.

a Christian Science
b Jehovah's Witnesses
c The Mormon Church
d Seventh-Day Adventist Church

Lengthy treatment of the history, source of authority and doctrines (God, Man, Christ, salvation, church and sacraments, eschatology) of each group. Sections on the distinctive traits of cults and how to approach cultists. A classic study. Much material on Seventh-Day Adventism, now seldom considered a cult.

35. Horowitz, Irving L., ed., *Science, Sin and Scholarship*, The MIT Press, 1978, hb, 290 pp., index

Moon, Rev. Sun Myung

A collection of essays by various writers who attempt to put the Unification Church movement into the perspective of American social history as well as the international political future. The editor of this impressive volume is a professor of sociology and political science at Rutgers. An interesting listing of charges against Moonies and an analytical response by a Pomona College (Calif.) philosopher. An excellent critique of Divine Principle theology in a National Council of Churches study document. 'We conclude that the Unification Church is not a Christian church because. . .' Much material on Moon's politics (activities of the Korean CIA, the Korea lobby, Moon's pro-Seoul activities and the civil liberties of sect members).

36. Irvine, William C., *Heresies Exposed*, Loizeaux Bros., 1917, pb.

a Christadelphianism
b Christian Science
c Freemasonry
d Jehovah's Witnesses
e The Mormon Church
f Spiritism
g Swedenborg, Emanuel
h Theosophy
i The Unitarian Church
j Unity School of Christianity

Brief, strongly worded critiques. A much-reprinted work, but dated. Some information on old groups now dead or dying (British Israelism, Buchmanism, Cooneyites).

37. Jones, D. Gareth, *Teilhard de Chardin: An Analysis and Assessment*, InterVarsity Press, 1969, pb, 72 pp.

de Chardin, Teilhard

Study of the mystical Catholic paleontologist who attempted to produce a scientifically acceptable phenomenology of the cosmos although his now-influential works were banned by the Roman Catholic Church until 1955. The author, a working biologist who is also a Christian, writes neither as a follower nor a debunker of de Chardin. Carefully annotated and readable.

38. Keel, John A., *The Eighth Tower*, Signet Books/New American Library, 1975, pb, 202 pp.

a Big Foot
b Loch Ness Monster
c Spiritism
d UFOs

Discussion of strange manifestations reputed in history and legend. Kell is a student of the 'paranormal' and a UFO advocate. An anti- Christian treatment, but interesting in that the Eighth Tower is Keel's code name for an evil consciousness which controls all of reality. Inventive speculation on the nature of the 'Devil' and the 'demonic' which Keel despairingly concludes to be the highest power. Keel's works are readable and fairly unbiased collections of occult and psychic happenings.

39. Koch, Kurt E., *Christian Counseling and Occultism*, Kregel Publications, 1972, pb, 338 pp., notes.

Occultic and psychic phenomena examined from theological and pscyhological perspectives

An attempt to balance the two extremes of denying the existence of the demonic and, on the other hand, demonising everything. Koch discusses the importance of distinguishing between demon possession and mental illness in therapy, as well as between mediumistic faculties and charismatic gifts. He talks about the fact, conquest and cure of demonic enslavement; and the need for genuine, spiritually gifted Christian counsellors rather than religiously disguised spiritistic mediums. A long study.

40. Koch, Kurt E., *The Devil's Alphabet*, Kregel Publications, 1971, pb, 156 pp.

a Anthroposophy
b Astrology
c Black magic
d Christian Science
e Clairvoyance
f Fetishes
g Firewalking
h Fortunetelling
i Freemasonry
j Ghosts
k Hypnosis
l Palmistry
m Spiritism
n Telepathy
o White magic
p Witchcraft
q Yoga

An A,B,C approach to superstitious and occult practices based on case studies from the author's counselling experience. The commentary, set in a European context, has a low-key style combined with a Christ-centred admonitory concern for the reader.

41. Koch, Kurt E., *Occult Bondage and Deliverance*, Kregel Publications, 1970, pb, 198 pp.

a Branham, William

b Counselling from the Scriptures
c Deliverance
d Distinction between disease and the demonic
e Healing (biblical and mediumistic)
f Occultism
g Psychic phenomena

A somewhat more popular approach than *Christian Counseling and Occultism*, with emphasis on a biblical view of healing and deliverance. Short discussion of Oral Roberts as a possibly mediumistic rather than a charismatic healer.

42. Langford, Harris, *Traps: A Probe of Those Strange New Cults*, Presbyterian Church in America, 1977, pb, 191 pp.
a Astrology
b Children of God
c Hare Krishna movement
d Occultism
e Scientology
f Transcendental Meditation
g The Unification Church
h The Way

Guide to nine cults that are relatively new or have experienced a revival. Study questions, attractive 8-1/2 x 11 plastic spiralbound format, imaginative often humorous graphics. Friendly, contemporary discussion for teenage Christians and their parents/teachers.

43. Levitt, Zola, *The Spirit of Sun Myung Moon*, Harvest House Publishers, 1976, pb, 127 pp.
Moon, Rev. Sun Myung

Personal narrative of the author's two visits to (and hostile behaviour at) Moon's New Yorker Hotel headquarters. Discusses Moon's views on America, Jesus and the future; largely based on material from the popular press: *Time, Jewish Digest*, newspapers. Reprint of an ex-Moonie's story from *Seventeen* magazine (1975).

44. Lewis, Gordon R., *What Everyone Should Know about Transcendental Meditation*, Regal Books/Division of G/L, 1975, pb, 92 pp., glossary.
Transcendental Meditation

A critique of TM, comparing Hindu and Christian views of questions such as 'What is Man's basic problem?' and 'How does one experience God?' The author is a professor at Conservative Baptist Theological Seminary, Denver. Includes a glossary comparing Christian and TM word usages.

45. Lightner, Robert P., *Meditation That Transcends*, Accent Books, 1976, pb, 64 pp., references.
Transcendental Meditation

Small booklet on TM, what it is, how it works and its dangers. Two chapters on 'transformational meditation' or 'biblical meditation' and how to appropriate God's gift of peace in a fast-moving age.

46. Malko, George, *Scientology: The Now Religion*, Delta Books/Dell Publishing Co., 1971, pb, 205 pp.
Scientology

A critical firsthand examination of The Founding Church of Scientology (official name): its theories and beliefs, how it operates, what it offers its disciples ('total freedom') and how much it costs (at least before the inflation of the '70s). The writer concludes that Scientology works because it is 'voluntary self-induced brainwashing. . . Scientology has been so shameless, so blatantly vulgar and commercial in telling its adherents all about The Truth and how to achieve it, that it has made a unique place for itself in our times.' An epilogue describes the resignation of Scientology's first 'Clear', who for many years had been a leading spokesperson for the movement.

47. Maloney, George A., *TM. and Christian Meditation*, Dove Publications, 1976, pb.

Transcendental Meditation

Small booklet discussing differences between prayer and TM. Proposes a Christian form of Transcendental Meditation: repeating the 'Jesus Prayer', or merely the name of Jesus, with cautions about psychic phenomena that may result. Maloney quotes St John of the Cross as saying: 'We must never rely upon them (psychic phenomena) or accept them, but must fly from them.'

48. Mangalwadi, Vishal, *The World of Gurus*, Vikas Publishing House Pvt Ltd, 1977, hb, 267 pp., index.

a. Chinmaya Mission
b. Chinmayanda, Swami
c. Desai, Sri Dattabal
d. Divine Life Society
e. Divine Light Mission
f. Hare Krishna movement
h. Muktananda, Swami
i. Nityananda, Swami
j. Radha Soami Satsang
k. Rajneesh
l. Sai Baba
m.Sikhs
n. Sivananda, Swami
o. Transcendental Meditation

The socio-historical background, intellectual impulses and religio-cultural aspirations that have produced the institution of the guru. The author describes his work as a 'researcher's quest for Truth in guruism', and as both a critique and an affirmation. One chapter on 'Evaluating Monistic Gurus' plus a final apologetic chapter on a unique figure, an invisible guru, who transforms his devotees into a 'new creation': Jesus. Well-indexed. Written from the context of Indian culture and primarily addressed to an Indian audience, but contains a wealth of insight and helpful information. Out of print.

49. Martin, Walter, *Essential Christianity*, Vision House Publishers, 1975, pb, 128 pp.

Orthodox Christian beliefs as contrasted with cultic beliefs

A short readable handbook of basic Christian doctrine by a writer who claims to 'understand the mind of a sceptic, the agnostic and the professional scoffer, since I have worn all their boots at one time or another and have followed the same old arguments to their dismal and fruitless conclusion'. Chapters on the inspiration of the Bible and the Trinity; Christ's deity, virgin birth, atonement and resurrection;

grace, works and spiritual gifts; hope and judgment; the error of universal salvation; the unanswerable argument (transformed lives). An attractive revision of a 1962 book.

50. Martin, Walter, *The Kingdom of the Cults*, Bethany Fellowship Press, 1965, hb, 443 pp., bibliography, index.

a. Anglo-Israelism (Herbert W. Armstrong)
b. Baha'i
c. Black Muslims
d. Christian Science and New Thought
e. Father Divine
f. Jehovah's Witnesses
g. The Mormon Church
h. Rosicrucianism
i. Seventh-Day Adventist Church
j. Spiritism (spiritualism)
k. Swedenborg, Emanuel
l. Theosophy
m. The Unitarian Church
n. Unity School of Christianity
o. Zen Buddhism

Historical analysis, theological evaluation and 'apologetic contrast' of major cults with biblical Christianity. Revised in 1968. The author sees Satan as the prime mover and architect of the cult systems. Summary chapters on 'The Kingdom of the Cults', 'Scaling the Language Barrier', 'The Psychological Structure of Cultism', 'The Jesus of the Cults', 'Cult-Evangelism-Mission Field on the Doorstep' and 'The Road to Recovery'.

51. McBeth, Leon, *Strange New Religions*, Broadman Press, 1977, pb, 154 pp., bibliography, notes.

a. Astrology
b. Children of God
c. Hare Krishna movement
d. Moon, Rev Sun Myung
e. Satanism
f. Scientology
g. Transcendental Meditation
h. Zen Buddhism

Short readable lectures on the new religions by a church historian at Southwestern Baptist Seminary. 'We cannot witness effectively to the fanatic cults,' he states, 'and all efforts to do so are a waste of time.'

52. Means, Pat, *The Mystical Maze*, Campus Crusade for Christ, 1976, pb, 275 pp., appendix.

a. Ananda Marga
b. Arica
c. Baba, Meher
d. Buddhism
e. Chinmoy, Sri
f. Gurdjieff
g. Hare Krishna movement
h. Healthy, Happy, Holy Organization
i. Martial arts
j. Nichiren Buddhism/Soka-gakkai
k. Ram Dass, Baba
l. Reincarnation
m. Sufis
n. Transcendental Meditation
o. The Unification Church

What is behind the shift toward Eastern religion? What is the secret of its appeal? Is there any way to communicate the gospel of Jesus Christ effectively to those who have adopted the Eastern mindset? A practical, evangelistic (rather than philosophical) attempt to answer such questions, with key-point summaries, 'how to's' and some graphics. Additional material, also evangelistically oriented, is provided in a 40-page supplementary-research section.

53. Miller, Calvin, *Transcendental Hesitation: A Biblical Appraisal of TM and Eastern Mysticism*, Zondervan Publishing House, 1977, pb, 185 pp., bibliography, glossary, notes.

Transcendental Meditation

Explains how TM and Christianity cannot be merged while being true to either. Points to Christianity as providing the key to reality and a satisfying world-and-life view. Chart comparing Eastern Movements: Krishna, TM and Zen. Out-of-the-ordinary chapters on altered states of consciousness and alternatives to TM.

54. Miller, Paul M., *The Devil Did Not Make Me Do It*, Herald Press, 1977, pb, 216 pp., bibliography, notes.

Christian deliverance from the enemy

A protest by a Mennonite leader about the many religious books today that picture the devil as 'too strong, as though he were really a second god running our universe.' The author, who has especially studied the practice of exorcism, spent several years in Africa. He emphasises that God wants persons to take responsibility for their own lives and offers a way of victory over the powers of evil.

55. Miller, William M., *A Christian's Response to Islam*, Presbyterian and Reformed Publishing Co., 1976, pb, 178 pp., bibliography.

Islam (Muslims)

Two chapters on the history, doctrines and practices of Islam; one on the differences between Islam and Christianity. The author, a Presbyterian missionary in Iran for over 40 years, gives four chapters to the difficulties Muslims face in becoming Christians and the need for a gospel outreach to the world's 600 million Muslims. Sensitive personal stories along with a theological approach.

56. Montgomery, John Warwick, *Principalities and Powers*, Bethany Fellowship Press, 1973, hb, 224 pp., appendix, illustrations, indices, notes.

a. Alchemy
b. Anthroposophy
c. Astrology
d. E.S.P.
e. Freemasonry
f. Kabala
g. Rosicrucianism
h. Satanism
i. Spiritism (spiritualism)
j. Tarot
k. Vampires (werewolves)
l. Witches
m. Zoroastrianism

A different, difficult, provocative approach to the occult, with an abundance of historical material to account for and interpret occult phenomena. The author's goal is to provide a scholarly work (20 pp. of footnotes) in contrast with the supposedly worthless character of other popular books on this subject — which he calls 'journalistic rehashings of yesterday's unscholarly popular treatments'. A barrier to readership is his complex, over-adjectival style (p.3 of chapter 1, for example, has a 150+ word sentence). Interesting illustrations and supplementary material.

57. Niles, D.T., *Buddhism and the Claims of Christ*, John Knox Press, 1967, pb, 87 pp., glossary.

Buddhism

An unusual attempt to state the Christian faith in the thought patterns of Buddhism. In this reprint of a 1946 work, the author covers the essentials of Christian faith in an effort to instruct catechumens whose background was Buddhist. Niles, a Ceylonese (Sri Lankan) Methodist minister, was internationally known as a speaker, author and leader in the Asian church. Out of print.

58. Noorbergen, Rene, *The Soul Hustlers*, Zondervan Publishing House, 1976, hb, 190 pp., notes.

a. Astrology
b. Dixon, Jeane
c. Psychics
d. Satanism
e. UFOs

Journalistic expose of today's invasion of Middle Ages superstition. Data based on interviews and lie detector/computer analysis of occult practitioners' answers to questions. The author discusses the traditional conflicts with biblical doctrine and develops his own Satanic-influence theory.

59. North, Gary, *None Dare Call It Witchcraft*, Arlington House Publications, 1976, hb, 253 pp., appendices, notes.

a. Alchemy
b. Arigo
c. Castaneda, Carlos
d. Cayce, Edgar
e. Cognition (pre-)
f. Croiset, Gerard
g. Dixon, Jeane
h. Dreams
i. Drugs (LSD)
j. Gnosticism
k. Healing (demonic)
l. Hoy, David
m. Hurkos, Peter
n. Kirlian photography
o. Plants, talking
p. Psychic photography
q. Psychics
r. Pyramidology
s. Sorcery
t. Spiritism
u. Table raising
v. Witchcraft
w. Yoga
x. Zen

A lengthy historical and contemplative study by a Reformed writer who relates occult revival in the West to cultural disintegration. 'Occult humanism is presently offering an alternative to . . . former materialistic humanists.' North attempts to demonstrate that the 'philosophy of witchcraft undergirds many movements that are not openly allied with the ancient arts of wicca . . . All hold to a view of man as a being wholly autonomous from the God of the Bible . . . The goal of this book is to present evidence of a set of phenomena that cannot be explained by the canons of Western rationalism.'

Although perhaps the author should be more sceptical of some of the phenomena he reports, the book is broad in material covered and interestingly written. The trite title is misleading. There are several good appendices, including 'Table Raising: Introduction to the Occult'.

60. Patton, John E., *The Case Against T.M. in the Schools*, Baker Book House, 1976, pb, 100 pp.
Transcendental Meditation
Research by a New Jersey lawyer documenting the religious nature of the Science of Creative Intelligence and Transcendental Meditation, which makes it illegal to be taught in public schools.

61. Petersen, William J., ed., *Astrology and the Bible*, Victor Books, 1972, pb, 32 pp.
Astrology
Booklet of brief essays by I.D.E. Thomas, Stuart Barton Babbage, Russell T. Hitt and the editor.

62. Petersen, William J., *Those Curious New Cults*, Pivot Books/Keats Publishing Co. Inc., 1975, pb, 272 pp., recommended further reading.
a. Armstrong, Herbert W.
b. Astrology
c. Baba, Meher
d. Baha'i
e. Black Muslims
f. Cayce, Edgar
g. Children of God
h. Divine Light Mission
i. Gurdjieff
j. Hare Krishna movement
k. I Ching
l. Moon, Rev Sun Myung
m. Satanism
n. Scientology
o. Spiritualism
p. Transcendental Meditation
q. Witchcraft
r. Zen Buddhism
Pungent journalistic accounts with a winsome Christian punch at the end of each. Brief but interestingly written; more than run-of-the-mill material.

63. Petersen, William J., *TM: A Do About Nothing*, Keats Publishing Co. Inc., 1976, pb. 106 pp., bibliography.
Transcendental Meditation
Well-researched, readable discussion of the Maharishi cult of the '70s. 'The physiological state in which a TM meditator places himself/herself is closely akin to that of a spiritualist medium during a seance as spirits are invited to appear.' Numerous quotes from Spiritual Counterfeits Project research. More detail on Maharishi's background and sayings than more popular treatments.

64. Reuter, Alan, *Who Says I'm OK*, Concordia Publishing House, 1974, pb, 125 pp, appendix.
Transactional Analysis
A Lutheran critique and adaptation of 'OKness psychology' to Christianity. Some reader involvement through questions, puzzles, songs; also a few graphics, poems and short stories. A generally helpful attempt to deal with a contemporary fad.

65. Ridenour, Fritz, ed., *So What's the Difference?*, Regal Books/G/L Publications, 1967, pb, 168 pp., bibliography.

a. Buddhism
b. Christian Science
c. Hinduism
d. Jehovah's Witnesses
e. The Mormon Church
f. The Unitarian Church

A brief attempt to examine differences between orthodox Christianity and other major religions/cults and see what can be learned from them. Light-hearted graphics with teenage appeal. Good questions and answers about the nature of Christianity in chapter 1.

66. Ropp, Harry L., *The Mormon Papers*, InterVarsity Press, 1977, pb, 100 pp., appendix, glossary, index, notes.

The Mormon scriptures

In response to Mormons' success in proselytising, a study of their teachings on God, Christ, salvation and the Bible. Evidence and theories on the origin of the Book of Mormon; the inauthenticity of key documents. One excellent chapter on how to witness to Mormons.

67. Schnell, William J., *How to Witness to Jehovah's Witnesses*, Baker Book House, 1975, pb, 157 pp.

Witnessing to Jehovah's Witnesses

From his background in training thousands of JWs in door-to-door witness, Schnell tries to help Christians in personal evangelism. Do's and don'ts on how to outmanouevre JW strategy. (Originally printed in 1961.)

68. Schnell, William J., *Thirty Years a Watchtower Slave*, Baker Book House, 1971, pb, 192 pp.

Jehovah's Witnesses

A detailed autobiographical account of the inner workings of the Jehovah's Witnesses, first in Europe and then in the US. The story more or less coincides with the growth of the cult, whose membership the writer regards as 'prisoners in a modern snake-pit'. He describes a seven-step indoctrination plan. His private book-selling business eventually clashed with JW leadership goals (1954).

69. Scott, R.D., *Transcendental Misconceptions*, Beta Books, 1978, pb, 227 pp., appendices, notes.

Transcendental Meditation

Autobiographically based discussion by a full- time TM teacher who spent six years in the movement. Chapters on how mantras are chosen, TM and demon possession, the author's disillusionment with its spiritual value, deceptive practices and financial inequity. Text of the initiator's loyalty pledge and training manual. Interesting appendices include accounts of ex-mediators, the scientific case against TM and an analysis of the Maharishi by the Spiritual Counterfeits Project.

70. Shah, Douglas, *The Meditators*, Logos International, 1975, pb, 147 pp.

a. Baba, Meher

b. Biofeedback
c. Buddhism
d. Confucianism
e. Islam
f. Reincarnation
g. Subud
h. Taoism
i. Transcendental Meditation
j. Yoga
k. Zen

A readable book by the grandson of an Indian Yogi. Good discussion of TM, its centuries-old roots in Hinduism and how it is being marketed and taught in the US. Several personal statements, one by Brooks Alexander of the Spiritual Counterfeits Project. One chapter on how to meditate as a Christian ('New Life Meditation').

71. Sharpe, Eric J., *Fifty Key Words: Comparative Religion*, John Knox Press, 1971, pb, 85 pp., index.
a. Animism
b. Astrology
c. Divination
d. Magic
e. Mysticism
f. Witchcraft

Elementary reference book for newcomers to the field. Defines technical terms and key concepts in Christian and non-Christian religions (1 or 2 pages on each). Helpful, although as in the study of comparative religion, there is a spirit of suspended judgment about the adequacy or inadequacy of specific beliefs.

72. Sire, James W., *The Universe Next Door*, InterVarsity Press, 1976, pb, 236 pp., index, notes.
a. Castaneda, Carlos
b. Eastern religion
c. Existentialism
d. The New Consciousness
e. Nihilism

An introduction to modern thinking subtitled *A Basic World View Catalog*. The editor of InterVarsity Press discusses the many universes around us: all fashioned by words and concepts that work together to form a particular world view. He describes historical roots and provides a critique of each. One superb chapter on 'The New Consciousness'.

73. Spiritual Counterfeits Project, *The God-Men*, SCP, 1978, pb, 80 pp., appendix, notes.
Witness Lee and the Local Church

An examination, in the light of scripture, of the history, doctrine and sociology of Witness Lee and the Local Church, based on Witness Lee's published works and on statements of Local Church spokesmen. Appendix on the 'Psychological Dynamic of the Local Church'. (Note: The revised, enlarged edition of *The God-Men: An Inquiry into Witness Lee and the Local Church* by Neil Duddy and the SCP, InterVarsity Press, 1980, pb, 156 pp.)

74. Spiritual Counterfeits Project, publisher, *TM in Court*, 1978, pb, 75 pp., appendix.
Transcendental Meditation

The complete text of Federal Court Judge H. Curtis Meanor's ruling against TM (in the case of Malnak v Maharishi Mahesh Yogi) as a violation of the establishment clause of the first amendment of the US Constitution. (The lawsuit was spearheaded both in research and financing by the SCP.) 'No inference was possible except that the teaching of SCI/TM and the *puja* are religious in nature; no other inference is "permissible" or "reasonable".'

75. Spotts, Michael, *Transcendental Meditation*, PO Box 367, Spanaway, WA 98387, USA, pb.
  Transcendental Meditation
A typewritten tract on TM: why it's here, what it claims to be, what it really is. Fair in content, but has too many errors (including the title misspelled on the cover) for general use.

76. Sumrall, Ken, *Manifested Sons: Truth and Error*, PO Box 3138, Pensacola, FL 32506, USA, 1972, pb, 38 pp.
  a. The Latter Rain Movement
  b. Manifested Sons of God
An attempt to counteract the ideas of the 'Manifested Sons' teachers among contemporary fundamentalist charismatics. Booklet mechanically reproduced in loose-leaf binder.

77. Swihart, Philip J., *The Edge of Death*, InterVarsity Press, 1978, pb, 96 pp.
  Thanatology
Excellent dicussion of the edge-of-death, beyond-death and out-of-body experiences furthered by the writings of Raymond A. Moody, Jr, Elisabeth Kubler-Ross and Robert A. Monroe. The conclusions of those researchers, which tie in with occult views, have disturbing implications for Christians. Swihart regards metaphysical encounters with 'spirit beings' (for example, with a relative now dead) as a probable impersonation by a demon who 'comes back to life'. Interesting analysis in one chapter of the above researchers' backgrounds and personal views.

78. Swihart, Philip J., *Reincarnation, Edgar Cayce and the Bible*, InterVarsity Press, 1975, pb, 57 pp., notes.
  a. Cayce, Edgar and the A.R.E.
  b. Reincarnation
Well-written booklet from a layperson's rather than a theologian's perspective about the attempt by Cayce's supporters to blend his views on reincarnation with Christianity. 'To accept Cayce's readings and teachings requires that one reject every major doctrine of the historic Christian faith', according to this author, a Colorado psychologist.

79. Van Baalen, Jan Kavel, *The Chaos of Cults*, Wm. B. Eerdmans Publishing Co., 1938, hb, 414 pp., bibliography.
  a. Armstrong, Herbert W.
  b. Astrology
  c. Baha'i
  d. Christian Science
  e. Jehovah's Witnesses
  f. The Mormon Church
  g. Rosicrucianism
  h. Spiritism
  i. Swedenborg, Emanuel
  j. Theosophy
  k. The Unitarian Church

l. Unity School of Christianity

An older, major study of the classic cults, enlarged and updated in 1962. Style is loose, subjective and fragmentary; has study questions but scanty specific documentation. Some chapters have discussions of the cult's view of Christian doctrines; some have conclusions. Four closing chapters are directed to Christians plus a long bibliography (now outdated).

80. Vosper, Cyril, *The Mind Benders*, Neville Spearman Ltd, 1971, hb, 187 pp., illustrated.

Scientology

A detailed account by an Englishman who spent 14 years in Scientology, then was declared an Enemy and Suppressive Person and ousted. Much information on Scientology's system of 'ethics', especially on ways of dealing with antagonists. An outline of the beliefs and practices and an explanation of the 'cops and robbers' vocabulary of this paramilitary organisation.

81. Wallis, Roy, ed., *Sectarianism*, Halstead Press/John Wiley and Sons, Inc., 1975, hb, 211 pp.

a. Aetherius Society
b. Hare Krishna movement
c. Scientology

Ten sociological essays, written largely by professors, analysing religious and nonreligious sects. Discusses the development, structure and inner workings of cults and sectarian movements and their impact on the secular domain. Scholarly but readable.

82. Weldon, John and Zola Levitt, *Is There Life After Death?*, Harvest House Publishers, 1977, pb, 147 pp.

Thanatology

Popular study of the contemporary fascination with death, 'after death' experiences, other OBEs and their parallels with occult writings and phenomena. Some comment on Elisabeth Kubler-Ross, Raymond Moody, Jr and Arthur Ford. Contains biblical analysis and some documentation in each chapter of popular press coverage of their reports.

83. Weldon, John and Zola Levitt, *The Transcendental Explosion*, Harvest House Publishers, 1976, pb, 218 pp., appendices, notes.

a. Reincarnation
b. Transcendental Meditation
c. Yoga

Easy-to-read discussion of TM's popularity, religious nature (Hindu), 'reconditioning of the brain' and antisocial and occult implications. Accounts of why various ex-meditators dropped out. Footnoted with popular references.

84. Weldon, John with Zola Levitt, *UFOS: What on Earth is Happening?*, Bantam Books, 1976, pb, 175 pp., appendices.

UFOs

Discussion of the writer's theory that UFOs are demon-caused, are related to the upcoming 'Tribulation' period and why they could not be devices of humanoids evolved elsewhere in the universe. Some documentation in each chapter of popular press coverage.

85. White, John, *Everything You Want to Know About TM – Including How to Do It*, Pocket Books, Inc./Simon and Shuster, Inc., 1976, pb, 191 pp., appendices, bibliography, glossary.
Transcendental Meditation
A secular investigation subtitled *A Look at Higher Consciousness and the Enlightenment Industry*. The author has a generally positive spirit toward the practice of TM, which he attempts to balance with caution and/or scepticism. 'If Maharishi is sufficient for your needs, fine. If he's not, pack up and move on.' Chapters on 'The Scientific Case Against TM', 'TM and Kundalini' and 'Higher Consciousness'.

86. Wilson, Clifford, *The Chariots Still Crash*, Signet Book/New American Library, 1975, pb, 182 pp., bibliography, notes.
Von Daniken
Further counter-arguments to Von Daniken's views. Comparison of early biblical material with Babylonian legends and some modest interpretations.

87. Wilson, Clifford and Weldon, John, *Close Encounters: A Better Explanation*, Master Books, 1978, pb, 354 pp., bibliography.
a. Extra terrestrials
b. Psychics
c. UFOs
A sequel-collaboration by two authors of earlier UFO books that expands their 'demonic theory' of UFO origins and relates to other occult phenomena. The sightings are seen as part of a pattern of Satanic deception to convince people, even Christian believers, that UFOs represent the universe's greatest powers and will be the means of ultimate deliverance from the world's chaos. 'Dabbling with... them involves... deadly risks, both spiritually and physically.' Unlike other books in this bibliography, these writers now include a disclaimer that they cannot vouch for the accuracy of the UFO tales they cite.

88. Wilson, Clifford, *Crash Go the Chariots*, Lancer Books, 1976, pb, 126 pp., bibliography, index.
a. Bermuda Triangle
b. The Pyramids
c. UFOs
d. Von Daniken's writings
An updating of a 1973 book (with some new material) by an Australian archaeologist/educator/journalist. An answer to Von Daniken, which discusses fallacies in his hypothesis concerning technical assistance to past civilisations by ancient astronauts – and the supposed biblical tie-ins – offers alternative explanations. Includes an interview with a Christian physicist, the late Frederick H. Giles (Univ. of South Carolina) concerning 'life on other planets'.

89. Wilson, Clifford, *Gods in Chariots and Other Fantasies*,

Creation-Life Publishers, 1975, pb 144 pp.
a. Pyramidology
b. Satan worship
c. UFOs
d. Von Daniken's writings

More of *Crash Go the Chariots, The Chariots Still Crash* and *U.F.O.s and Their Mission Impossible,* generally categorised as forms of 'opposition to the power of Almighty God.'

90. Wilson, Clifford, *The Occult Explosion*, Master Books, 1976, pb.
a. Astrology
b. Black Magic
c. Chinmoy, Sri
d. Divine Light Mission
e. E.S.P.
f. Exorcism
g. Fortunetelling
h. Geller, Uri
i. Hare Krishna movement
j. Hypnotism
k. Palmistry
l. Psychic phenomena
m. Psychometry
n. Seances
o. Spiritism
p. Transcendental Meditation
q. Witchcraft

Brief discussion of various aspects of the penetration of the West by the East, interpreted as a 'demonic explosion'. Satanic powers, fearing that their time is fast running out, are engaging in a desperate effort to defeat God's purposes for humanity.

91. Wilson, Clifford, *U.F.O.s...and Their Mission Impossible,* Word of Truth Productions, Inc., 1974, pb, 243 pp., appendices, bibliography, indices, notes.
UFOs

Discussion of UFO sightings, the credibility of witnesses, contacts made and spacenappings. The author, a convinced reporter, suggests their association with demon activity rather than interplanetory visitors. An extensive discussion of the film *The Exorcist* in the appendix.

92. Wright, J. Stafford, *Christianity and the Occult*, Moody Press, 1971, pb, 160 pp.
a. Occultism
b. Spiritism

A possibly overcredulous consideration of unusual psychic/occultic happenings in light of the total revelation given in scripture. The author expresses concern that the flood of publications on this subject might incite rather than deter interest in spiritism. 'Normally a human being is a defended castle, but any trafficking with the spirit world lets down the drawbridge... No one who has read this book could now dabble in occultism innocently.' A sensible final chapter, 'What Should I Do?', is directed to those who are tempted in this area.

93. Wright, J. Stafford, *Mind, Man and the Spirits*, Zondervan Publishing House, 1968, pb, 190 pp., appendix, bibliography, index.
a. Astral projection
b. Auras
c. Clairvoyance
d. Cognition (pre-)
e. Cognition (retro-)
f. Demon possession
g. Dreams

h. Firewalking
i. Healing
j. Levitation
k. Miracles
l. Poltergeists
m.Psychometry
n. Reincarnation
o. Spiritualism
p. Telepathy

A revision of a 1955 book, *What is Man?*, which is a more sophisticated and theological approach than most books on this subject. Chapters on the Christian belief in transcendence and immanence, the view of human nature in depth psychology, the mind in relation to space/time, the significance of beauty, miracles, the biblical view of Man, revelation and inspiration, in addition to sections on occultism, spiritism and reincarnation. Out of print.

94. Yamauchi, Edwin M., *Jesus, Zoroaster, Buddha, Socrates, Mohammed*, InterVarsity Press, 1971, pb, 48 pp., notes, recommended further reading.
a. Buddha
b. Mohammed
c. Socrates
d. Zoroastrianism

Small booklet with short summaries of documentary sources, birth and family, life and teachings, death and relation to the deity of the above five religious leaders. Evangelistic conclusion. (Revised in 1972.)

95. Yamamoto, J. Isamu, *The Puppet Master*, InterVarsity Press, 1977, pb, 136 pp., notes.
Moon, Rev. Sun Myung

The most thorough and insightful Christian critique of Moon and the Unification Church, with an excellent chapter on a Christian response to the Moonies. The author, a researcher with the Spiritual Counterfeits Project, has been active in such witness. 'If we encounter them as enemies on a battlefield, if we pit our beliefs against their beliefs, if with our desire to be right we overrule the Spirit's love for them as lost children, then whether or not we win or lose the battle, we lose the war. And worse: They will lose all.' Also, a thoughtful section on deprogramming.

96. Zaehner, R.C., *Zen, Drugs and Mysticism*, Vintage Books, Random House, Inc., 1974, pb, 223 pp., index.
a. de Chardin, Teilhard
b. Drugs (LSD)
c. Mysticism
d. Zen

A learned and sophisticated discussion of the relationship between drug-induced numinous consciousness and the mystical experiences of remarkable figures in all the world's religions. Based on BBC lectures given in 1970, the author brings together extensive quotations from significant 20th-century writers. Zaehner is well-known as a scholar of comparative religion in the Roman Catholic tradition. His understanding of Christianity is far from evangelicalism on most points, but his book is distinguished by an illuminating and trenchant chapter on Teilhard de Chardin.

Topical Index for Appendix A

Appendix B

Resources relevant to religious cults in Australia

compiled by J.L.F. Buchner

Australian ministries

Ambassador Research International (J.L.F. Buchner, Lecturer, Macarthur Institute of Higher Education, PO Box 108, Milperra, NSW 2214)

Specialising in the Worldwide Church of God and its offshoots, and the scientific study of new religious movements. Publications include *Armstrongism in Australia* and *Armstrongism Bibliography.*

Australian Christian Research Ministries (Laci Csont, Director, PO Box 311, Sutherland, NSW 2232)

Specialising in Jehovah's Witnesses and Mormons, as well as others. Publishes monthly newsletter and conducts Cults Clinics upon invitation by local churches.

Concerned Christians Growth Ministries (Adrian Van Leen, Director, PO Box 6, North Perth, WA 6006)

General literature, newsletter and seminars. Publications include *O is for Orange* (on Rajneesh).

Escape to Life Mission (Loraine Sampson, Director, PO Box 36, Hamilton Hill, WA 6163)

'Half-way house' for ex-cultists. Recommended by Mandate.

Good News Down Under (Richard Ansoul, Director, PO Box 221, Baulkham Hills, NSW 2153)

Counselling by Baptist minister. Literature includes *Good News for Jehovah's Witnesses*, (Stuckey) and *Good News for Mormons* (Bracht).

Good News Unlimited (PO Box 1603, Hornsby Northgate, NSW 2077)

Publishes monthly newsletter promoting Gospel among Seventh Day Adventists. Publications include *Good News for Adventists* by Desmond Ford.

McGregor Ministries (PO Box 538, Prospect East, SA 5082)
Specialising in Jehovah's Witnesses. Publishes newsletter. Distributes tapes and tracts by Lorri McGregor, of Canada.

Mandate Ministries (Fred Grigg, Director, PO Box 31, Greenacre, NSW 2190)
Evangelical ministry, with expertise in Jehovah's Witnesses. Conducts seminars upon invitation by local churches. Publications include *The Answer to the Cult Explosion*.

Australian publications

Allan, John, Butterworth, John, and Langley, Myrtle, *A Book of Beliefs*, Sutherland, NSW: Albatross Books, 1983 (includes reprint of Butterworth, below).

Butterworth, John, *Cults and New Faiths*, Sutherland, NSW: Albatross Books, 1981 (reprinted in Allan et al., above)

Grigg, Fred R., *The Answer to the Cult Explosion*, Mandate Ministries, PO Box 31, Greenacre, NSW 2190

New South Wales Anti-Discrimination Board, *Discrimination and Religious Conviction*, NSW Government Information Centre, 55 Hunter Street, Sydney, NSW 2000

Tarling, Lowell, *The Edges of Seventh Day Adventism*, Galilee Publications, Barraga Bay, Bermagui South, NSW 2547, 1981

Van Sommers, Tess, *Religions in Australia*, Rigby, Adelaide: 1966 (Out of print)

Wheat, H. Colin, *The Shattered Cross in Australia*, 1982, Western Australian Churches of Christ minister (The bookroom, Shop 8, Endeavour Arcade, 360 The Kingsway, Caringbah, NSW 2229)

Australian periodicals

Anon. 'The new sects', *Current Affairs Bulletin* 58(4):4-27, September 1981

Bracht, John, 'Mormonism: magnificent delusion', *Australian Church Record*, 1822:4-5 (22 April 1985)

Dent, Owen, 'Church-sect typologies in the description of religious groups', *Australian and New Zealand Journal of Sociology* 6(1):10-27 (April 1970)

Horwitz, Tony, 'The cult culture', *Sydney Morning Herald Saturday Review* (21 September 1985); p.42

Hunter, Ian, 'Sects and cults I', *St Mark's Review* 107:27-36 (September 1981)

Ryan, Noel, 'Sects and cults II', *St Mark's Review* 107:37-44 (September 1981)

Stuckey, Warren, 'Leaving the Jehovah's Witnesses', *Australian Church Record* 1834:6-7 (23 September 1985)

Van Leen, Adrian, 'False Christs and farcical creeds', *On Being* 9(9):18-20 (October 1982)

World Evangelisation, 'The New Age movement examined', *Australian Church Record* 1838:11 (18 November 1985)

Audiovisual resources

Australian Religious Film Society
PO Box 97, North Ryde, NSW 2113 (02-888 2511)

The Counterfeits (Film Educators 1981, Colour 45 minutes)
16mm film and Beta/VHS
The Cult Explosion (New Liberty 1979, Colour 40 minutes)
Beta/VHS

Gospel Film Ministries
309 Pitt Street (8th Floor), Sydney, NSW 2000 (02-267 3911)

The Cult Explosion (New Liberty 1979, Colour 55 minutes)
16mm film only
Deceived 1 [on Jonestown] (Gospel Films 1980, Colour 45 minutes)
16mm film only
Deceived 2 (Gospel Films 1983, Colour 45 minutes)
16mm film only

Gods of the New Age (Jeremiah Films 1984, Colour 90 minutes)
16mm film only
The Godmakers [Mormons] (Jeremiah Films 1983, Colour 55 minutes)
16mm film and VHS video
Temple of the Godmakers (Jeremiah Films 1985, Colour 30 minutes)
16mm film only

Appendix C

Resources relevant to religious cults in Britain

compiled by Deo Gloria Outreach

British ministries

Breda Centre (Jim McCormick, c/o 12 Ballynahinch Road, Carryduff, Belfast, BT8 8DN)

Extensive books and tracts on cults; seminars; information; counselling. Publications include: *Great Joy* magazine and *Christ, the Christian and Freemasonry.*

Christian Information Outreach (Eric Clarke, 92 The Street, Boughton, near Faversham, Kent, ME13 9AP).

Information on new and old extreme religious groups; teaching/training in churches, Bible colleges; seminars; counselling for parents/relatives, and cult members if desired. Publications include: *Awareness*, a quarterly journal, and *Aid to Watchtower Understanding*, a manual.

Christian Response to the Occult, (Tom Poulson, PO Box 150, Bromley, Kent, BR1 1BY)

A service to warn and inform about the dangers of occult involvement.

Deo Gloria Outreach (Joy Caton, 7 London Road, Bromley, Kent, BR1 1BY).

Information to Christian and secular public of the growing challenge posed by pseudo-Christian and quasi religions. Advice and counsel arranged.

Dialogcentre UK (Christian Szurko, c/o 19 Newstead, Hatfield, Herts, AL10 9DH)

Advicc and counselling for families of members, voluntary counselling and rehabilitation for members; presentations in RE classes; lectures at colleges, universities and churches; training for individuals and groups; information on new religions.

Echoes of Utah (John M. Cuthbert, PO Box 12, Northampton)

Evangelism and counsel to cult members; church teaching/information; literature and cassettes; seminars.

Ex-Mormons for Jesus (Terry Crompton, 68 Langley Walk, Crawley, W.Sussex, RH11 7LR)

Literature and information on Mormons.

Help Jesus (Paul Alcuri, PO Box 28, Canterbury, Kent, CT1 1AA)

Tracts for Jehovah's Witnesses.

Reach Out (Doug Harris, PO Box 34, Twickenham, TW2 7EG)

General literature and information on many cults, in-depth on Jehovah's Witnesses; evangelism to cult members; seminars; link-up of Christians involved in cult ministries, and those able to counsel cult members and families. Publications include a quarterly newsletter and a manual, *Awake to the Watchtower.*

Publications available in Britain

For a list of recent publications, see *Update*, the quarterly journal published by The Dialog Center, Katrinebjergvj, 46, DK-8200 Aarhus N, Denmark. Analytical articles; discussion of new religions; dialogue, in print, between readers with a Christian worldview and those participating in new religions.

General

A Lion Handbook: *The World's Religions*, Lion Publishing.

Allan, John, Butterworth, John, and Langley, Myrtle, *A Book of Beliefs*, Lion Publishing.

Allan, John, *Shopping for a God*, IVP.

Anderson, Sir Norman, *The World's Religions*, IVP.

Boalen, Van, *The Chaos of Cults*, Eerdmans.

Breese, David, *Know the Marks of Cults*, Victor Books.

Bussell, Harold, *Unholy Devotion: Why Cults Lure Christians*, Zondervan.

Enroth, Ron et al, *A Guide to Cults and New Religions*, IVP.

Enroth, Ron, *Lure of the Cults*, Christian Herald Books.

Enroth, Ron, *Youth, Brainwashing and the Extremist Cults*, Paternoster Press.

Guiness, Os, *Dust of Death*, IVP.

Martin, Walter, *The Kingdom of the Cults*, Bethany House.

Martin, Walter, *The New Cults*, Vision House.

Mehta, Gita, *Karma Cola*, Jonathan Cape.

Sire, James, *The Universe Next Door*, IVP.

Sire, James, *Scripture Twisting*, IVP.

After Life
Albrecht, Mark, *Reincarnation*, IVP.

Brooke, Tal, *The Other Side of Death*, Tyndale House.

Swihart, P., *The Edge of Death*, IVP.

Astrology
Bjornstad, James, *Stars, Signs and Salvation in the Age of Aquarius*, Dimension Books.

Bahai
Beckwith, Francis, *Bahai*, Bethany House.

Children of God
Davis, Deborah, *Children of God: The Inside Story*, Zondervan.

Christian Aberrations
Barrs, Jerram, *Freedom and Discipleship*, IVP.

Bulle, Florence, *God Wants You Rich and Other Enticing Doctrines*, Bethany House.

Magliato, Joe, *The Wall Street Gospel*, Harvest House.

Walker, Andrew, *Restoring the Kingdom*, Hodder and Stoughton.

Eastern
Allan, John, *Yoga*, IVP.

Brooke, Tal, *Riders of the Cosmic Circuit*, Lion Publishing.

Clements, R.D., *God and the Gurus*, IVP.

Guptara, Prabhu, *Indian Spirituality*, Grove Books.

Maharaj, R.R. and Hunt, Dave, *Death of a Guru*, Hodder and Stoughton.

Means, Pat, *The Mystical Maze*, Campus Crusade.

Freemasonry

Decker, Ed., *The Question of Freemasonry*, Saints Alive.

Knight, Stephen, *The Brotherhood*, Granada.

Islam

McDowell and Gilchrist, *The Islam Debate*, Campus Crusade.

Jehovah's Witnesses

Bjornstad, J., *Counterfeits at Your Door*, Regal Books.

Duggar, Gordon E., *Jehovah's Witnesses: Watch Out for the Watchtower*, Baker Book House.

Gruss, Edmund, *Apostles of Denial*, Baker Book House.

Gruss, Edmund, *The Jehovah's Witnesses and Prophetic Speculation*, Presbyterian and Reformed Publishing Co.

Hoekema, A.A., *Jehovah's Witnesses*, Paternoster Press.

Magnani, Duane, *Watchtower Files*, Bethany House.

Martin, W. and Klann, N., *Jehovah of the Watchtower*, Bethany House.

Morey, Robert, *How to Answer a Jehovah's Witness*, Bethany House.

Schnell, William, *How to Witness to Jehovah's Witnesses*, Baker Book House.

Mormonism

Geer, Thelma, *Mormonism, Mama and Me*, Calvary Missionary Press.

McElveen, Floyd, *Mormon Revelations of Convenience*, Bethany Fellowship.

Martin, Walter, *The Maze of Mormonism*, Vision House.

Morey, Robert, *How to Answer a Mormon*, Bethany House.

Ropp, Harry, *The Mormon papers*, IVP.

New Age
Houghton, John, *The Healthy Alternative*, Kingsway.

Reisser, P.C., Reisser, T.K. and Weldon, John, *The Holistic Healers*, IVP.

Occult
Allan, John, *Dealing with Darkness*, Hansel Press.

Korem, Danny and Meier, Paul, *The Fakers*, Baker Book House.

Unger, Merrill, *What Demons Can Do to Saints*, Moody Press.

Weldon, John, *Encounters with UFO's*, Harvest House Publishers.

Weldon, John and Bjornstad, James, *Playing with Fire*, Moody Press.

School of Economic Science
Hovnam, Peter and Hogg, Andrew, *Secret Cult*, Lion Publishing.

Spiritualism
Lewis, Gordon R., *The Bible, the Christian and Spiritualists*, Presbyterian and Reformed Publishing Co.

Gasson, Raphael, *The Challenging Counterfeit*, Bridge Publishing Co.

Transcendental Meditation
TM in Court, Spiritual Counterfeits Project.

Bjornsted, James, *The Transcendental Mirage*, Bethany Fellowship.

Haddon, D., *TM Wants You!*, Baker Book House.

Unification Church
Bjornstad, James, *Sun Myung Moon and the Unification Church*, Bethany House.

The Way International
Williams, J.L., *Victor Paul Wierwille and The Way International*, Moody Press.

Worldwide Church of God
Martin, Walter, *Herbert Armstrong and the Radio Church of God*, Bethany Fellowship.

Audiovisual resources

Anchor Recordings, 72 The Street, Kennington, Ashford, Kent, TN24 9HS (0233 20958).

Christian Video Experience, 6 Cecil Way, Bromley, Kent, BR2 7JU (01-462 5934).

Christian World Centre, PO Box 30, 123 Deansgate, Manchester, M60 3BX (061 834 6060).

Evangelical Film Fellowship, Moulsham Mill Centre, Parkway, Chelmsford, Essex, CM2 7PX (0245 25 2414).

Highland Christian Video Fellowship, 47 Telford Road, Inverness, Scotland, IV3 6JA (0463 224788).

International Films, 235 Shaftesbury Avenue, London WC2H 8EL, (01 836 2255).

Appendix D:

Christian orthodoxy and deviation

DEGREE OF DEVIATION		GENERAL CHARACTERISTICS	DOCTRINE OF THE TRINITY	DOCTRINE OF JESUS
	ORTHODOX	Safety zone Commonly accepted doctrine	One God in three distinct persons; three in one and one in three	Jesus both God and man and a member of the Trinity. The only begotten Son of God. The only way to salvation.
			INNER PERIMETER OF SAFETY	
	UNORTHODOX	Safety questionable Questionable doctrine	One God who manifests himself in the Father, Son and Holy Spirit, i.e. one God in three manifestations	Denial of full deity or humanity of Jesus. Belief that others may possibly be saved without knowing Jesus.
			OUTER PERIMETER OF SAFETY	
	MILDLY HERETICAL	Dangerous Clearly false doctrine	Denial of the full deity of Father, Son and Holy Spirit	Believes it is not necessary to know Jesus to be saved. Other prophets can bring salvation.
	STONGLY HERETICAL		← Denial that Jesus is God; denial that Jesus came in the flesh; denial that Jesus both man and God →	

For most people, the term *cult* conjures up images of arcane, secretive societies whose members hold bizarre beliefs and swear allegiance to a living guru or self-proclaimed messiah. We found something like this to be the case in most major cults. *But we were surprised to find that the majority of cult groups, including many we had never heard of before, were fundamentalist Christian sects apparently employing sophisticated mind-control techniques.*

Thirty out of forty-eight cults we surveyed emerged out of this traditional branch of Christianity . . . They also rated higher than all cults except Scientology in combined long-term effects and average rehabilitation time (nineteen months).*

* From 'Information Disease: Have Cults created a New Mental Illness?', by Flo Conway and Jim Siegleman (*Science Digest*, Hearst Magazines, New York, 1982, p.92).